LISA'S STORY

LISA'S STORY

Tom Batiuk

Creator of *Funky Winkerbean*

A PERIGEE BOOK

NABCO reminds readers that Lisa's experience with breast cancer and her resulting medical decisions are based on her individual case and choices, and that each woman's experience with this disease will be different. Decisions about breast cancer risk, detection and treatment should be made based on current medical information, in consultation with a physician or other qualified health professionals.

A Perigee Book
Published by The Berkley Publishing Group
A division of Penguin Putnam Inc.
375 Hudson Street
New York, New York 10014

Copyright © 2000 by Batom, Inc.
Cover design by Dawn Velez-LeBron
Text design by Tiffany Kukec

First edition: October 2000

Published simultaneously in Canada.

The Penguin Putnam Inc. World Wide Web site address is
http://www.penguinputnam.com

Library of Congress Cataloging-in-Publication Data

Batiuk, Tom.
    Lisa's story / Tom Batiuk.
        p. cm.
    ISBN 0-399-52666-8
    1. Breast—Cancer—Comic books, strips, etc. I. Title.

RC280.B8 B375 2000
616.99'449—dc21
                                                        00-055772

Printed in the United States of America

10   9   8   7   6   5   4   3   2   1

For Cathy, my Lisa

CONTENTS

A Note from Tom Batiuk

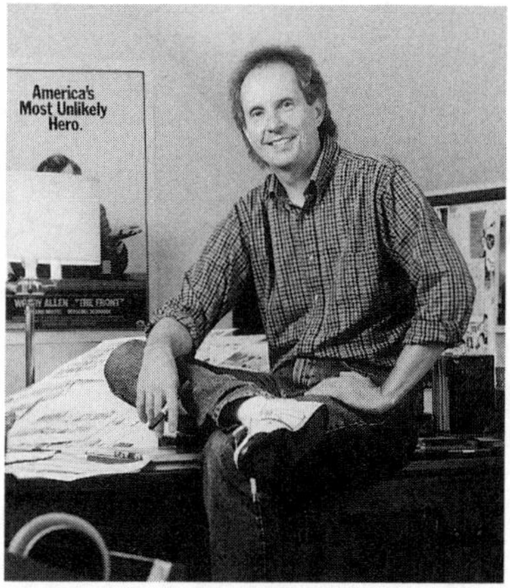
America's
Most Unlikely
Hero.

Ever since my characters in *Funky Winkerbean* outgrew their high school beginnings, I've found myself as a writer having to grow along with them as they entered an unpredictable adult world. With each brush of reality that the characters encountered, I learned more about their strengths and weaknesses and marveled at how they changed and how much more interesting they became. The relationship between Les and Lisa, in particular, had already evolved a lot even before I decided to test it with the specter of breast cancer.

To do that, I had to make the effort to learn about, understand and inhabit that other world, and immerse myself in a totally different frame of reference. I worked on the story for about four years, outside of the ongoing *Funky* strip, which allowed me the time to do the necessary research, writing and rewriting that such a subject called for without having to be concerned with looming deadlines.

In a foreword to a collection of 1986 strips about Lisa's teen pregnancy, I expressed concern over whether a comic strip was the proper place to explore such a topic. Since then, my characters have shown me that the comics form is indeed capable of carrying the weight of mature expression. It allows us to wrestle with ideas in the world of fantasy before bumping into them in the gritty world of reality. Although there is no cure for life, interesting, humorous and useful descriptions of our struggles can, and I think do, make a difference.

It is to that thought that *Lisa's Story* is dedicated.

—Tom Batiuk, 1998

Lisa's Story

Who Is _Funky Winkerbean_?

Tom Batiuk spent several years as a high school teacher before creating _Funky Winkerbean,_ the celebrated comic strip distributed to more than four hundred newspapers nationwide. His years of teaching crystallized his interest in drawing a comic strip about teenage students, and he began drawing a panel for the teen page of the _Elyria Chronicle-Telegram_ in 1970. That led to the creation of _Funky Winkerbean_ in 1972, which was named with the help of students in his art class. The comic strip began as a laugh-a-day look at high school life and has matured into a series of real-life stories, highlighting such sensitive social issues as cancer, teen-dating abuse, teen suicide, guns in school and teen pregnancy. Batiuk's bold characterizations and dramatic plots engage his readers—teens, parents and educators alike—in stories with which they can identify.

Realizing that there are many strips on the comics page for readers interested in a fantasy world, Batiuk strives to provide an alternative by creating more powerful and real stories. In 1986, he endeavored to capture the struggles of real teenagers to cope with the most sensitive of issues. It was with more than a little trepidation that Batiuk set out to explore the issue of teen pregnancy. The story line received widespread public support, generating more than sixty thousand requests for reprints from teens, parents, teachers, and community groups across the country. In 1987, Batiuk did a story on two students with dyslexia. In 1994, Batiuk addressed the frightening issue of guns in the classroom and in 1999, he took on breast cancer. Batiuk has won accolades and awards from his peers as well as from educators and professional and civic organizations across the country for his outstanding treatment of serious social issues.

Lisa's Story

A Husband's Loving Wish

Dear Mr. Batiuk:

You stopped my morning paper reading in its tracks with the news that *Funky Winkerbean* will address breast cancer during the next six months.

My wife of fifty-five years, now bald from radiation for multiple metastases from her 1995 breast cancer, unknowingly to her has given me a problem I haven't been able to deal with properly—no, not properly—but lovingly. I want her to know how inadequate and uncomfortable I feel in my attempts to have her know how much I care, how much I want to talk with her about her feelings, how much I am on her side. I try constantly—I pray constantly to become more a part of her difficulty. I never know if I get through to her.

Please, have *Funky* help me out. I feel sure there are multitudes of caring husbands who are nervously shifting from one foot to another wondering what to do. We love our wives and the idea of having to give them up is much more than we can handle—especially when we feel they do not know how much we care. You would think that after forty-six and a half years of family medical practice, it would have long ago have given me multiple examples of how to mentally, emotionally and physically put my arms around her, have her know how much I care, want to help and want her to open up and talk to me about her lethal burden so we could share while holding her in my arms.

Sincerely,
W. J. Hagood, Jr., M.D.

Lisa's Story

Can Cancer Tickle the Funny Bone?

Five hundred women started today by brushing their teeth and chugging their coffee, but by sundown their lives will be forever changed, since today they will learn they have breast cancer. Cancer has never been a subject that tickles the funny bone, and because breast cancer is the most common form of cancer in women in the United States, this topic is especially sobering. As the leading nonprofit information and education resource on the disease, the National Alliance of Breast Cancer Organizations (NABCO) would never suggest that breast cancer is a laughing matter. Like the main character in *Lisa's Story,* what we do suggest is that every woman put her fears aside, learn the facts and become proactive against this disease, and that she keep her sense of humor, and her perspective, intact. Women tell us that when they do this, what they discover is surprisingly reassuring, and very different from what they had suspected—and feared. The reality of breast cancer today reflects tremendous scientific progress and medical promise—it's no longer your mother's disease. Facing breast cancer a generation ago, women often lost their lives, and always lost their breasts. They seldom talked about it, denying themselves the comforts of a sisterhood of survivors that now numbers two million, and forgoing the emotional support that can be crucial to recovery. In their silence, our mothers also unintentionally perpetuated the misinformation and myths that can surround this disease.

Now, we talk about breast cancer openly, and there is good news. With early detection and prompt treatment, 97 percent of women diagnosed today will be alive and well in five years. Almost every woman whose breast cancer is found early can choose treatment that preserves the breast, and those who cannot are often candidates for skillful breast reconstruction.

Every woman is at risk for breast cancer, not just those with a family history of the disease. And while the diagnosis is most likely in women who are in their fifties, sixties and beyond, younger women are increasingly joining the ranks. Because breast cancer in women in their forties and even in their thirties is no longer such a rare event, every young woman should follow a breast health program. Every woman should be getting a thorough breast exam every year by a doctor or nurse starting at age twenty. Starting at age forty, a yearly screening mammogram (a breast X ray) should be added to the annual breast exam—or possibly earlier if a close blood relative has had breast cancer, especially if she was diagnosed before age fifty. With the majority of women now getting regular breast exams, yearly mammograms starting at age forty and checking their own breasts, cancers are being found sooner, at smaller sizes. As the enemy is shrinking, it is becoming less lethal.

Lisa's Story

Early detection offers the best chance to beat breast cancer, however, it is access to good information that guides a woman through treatment and helps her through its many decisions. So readers can accomplish this, we have added useful information from NABCO to *Lisa's Story*. As she navigates the breast cancer journey, Lisa experiences her share of funny, very real moments, but in her actions Lisa offers this wise guidance: be thoughtful, and do your research. Using creative and entertaining channels like comics is often the best way to educate and *Lisa's Story* is a welcome new tool in the fight against breast cancer.

Excerpts from the *NABCO Breast Cancer Resource List*—books, brochures, hot lines, support groups, web sites and more—organized in the order of Lisa's story, pave a clear path of good information to follow. We share what's important, what to expect and how to prioritize, each step of the way. Many of the resources listed are free of charge, and you can always learn more by calling NABCO toll free at (888) 80-NABCO, or by visiting www.nabco.org. NABCO is grateful that a portion of the sales of *Lisa's Story* will support our information and education programs, and we thank Lisa, Tom Batiuk and our friends at King Features and Penguin Putnam Inc. for making this possible.

Lisa shares her story with five hundred women every day, every month of the year in the United States. At the pace medical research is moving, soon we will be able to prevent the disease in the first place, and promise every woman who is diagnosed today a certain cure. But until then, early detection and good sources of information are a woman's best defense. If you can laugh, and keep your sense of humor, it's a definite plus. Having a husband around like Les, and a friend like *Funky Winkerbean* can't hurt either.

Amy S. Langer, Executive Director*
National Alliance of Breast Cancer Organizations (NABCO)
May 2000

*Amy Langer is a fifteen-year breast cancer survivor who was diagnosed when she was thirty years old.

Lisa's Story

"Lisa's Story made me laugh,

it made me cry, and most importantly,

it gave me hope."

JUST BECAUSE THE GAME IS OVER DOESN'T MEAN WE HAVE TO STOP PLAYING...

I COULD STILL THROW A FEW PASSES YOUR WAY...

AS LONG AS YOU PROMISE THERE'LL BE PLENTY OF HOLDING PENALTIES...

1-20

ARE YOU SURE YOU'RE OKAY?

I'M FINE... I THINK I WAS JUST A LITTLE SORE FROM THE FOOTBALL GAME!

CARE TO HIT THE TEAM SHOWERS?

THANKS ...BUT I THINK I'M GOING TO NAP A BIT!

1-21

I LEFT SOME HOT WATER FOR YOU, KID!

THANKS!

1-22

"I've fallen in love with this comic.

It is an amazing piece of work."

SELF-EXAMINATION (BSE)

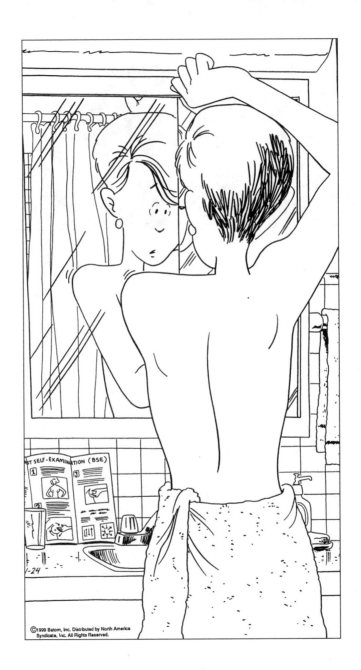

HAVE A GOOD DAY!

YEAH, YOU, TOO, KID!

I'D LIKE TO SEE THE DOCTOR AS SOON AS I CAN!

1-25

LEESE... I'M HOME!

LISA?

1-26

SO LISA WENT TO SEE A DOCTOR WITHOUT TELLING YOU? SAY, YOU DON'T SUPPOSE SHE'S...

WELL, WE WEREN'T PLANNING ON IT, BUT YOU NEVER KNOW...

'WHY ELSE WOULD SHE DO THAT?'

IT FEELS LIKE A CYST... A LOT OF WOMEN HAVE THEM... WE'LL SEND YOU FOR SOME MAMMOGRAMS!

MEDICAL BUIL
C. PARKS MD
L. SMITH MD
J. JOHNSON MD

1-27

■ 5

"I want you to know that <u>Lisa's Story</u> is the most accurate portrayal we have ever seen of the emotions surrounding breast cancer, especially the humor."

"Your insight into the emotions, including the reactions of friends and family, is totally on target. Not only is <u>Lisa's Story</u> accurate, but you use humor to its best advantage."

THANKS FOR TAKING A WALK WITH ME, LES!

I JUST COULDN'T FACE ALL OF THE BUSTLE AND GOOD CHEER AT MONTONI'S RIGHT NOW!

JUST BECAUSE THEY SPOTTED SOMETHING ON YOUR MAMMOGRAM DOESN'T NECESSARILY MEAN THAT IT'S SOMETHING BAD...

IN FACT, DR. PARKS HIMSELF SAID THAT MOST OF THESE THINGS ARE BENIGN!

AND EVEN IF IT'S NOT... WE'VE LIVED THROUGH STUFF LIKE THIS BEFORE, AND WE CAN DO IT AGAIN!

YOU SURE KNOW HOW TO SAY THE RIGHT THING AT THE RIGHT TIME... YOU'VE CONVINCED ME!

NOW I WISH I COULD CONVINCE MYSELF!

1-31

One week later

HOW DO WE KNOW THAT THIS SURGEON WE'RE GOING TO SEE IS A GOOD ONE?

I'M SURE HE IS... BESIDES, DIDN'T DR. PARKS SAY THAT DR. RAL IS THE SURGEON HE'D WANT <u>HIS</u> WIFE TO SEE?

2-1

MAYBE WE SHOULD'VE ASKED HOW HE AND HIS WIFE WERE GETTING ALONG!

BASED ON YOUR X-RAYS, MRS. MOORE, AND MY EXAMINATION... I'D HAVE TO CONCLUDE THAT...

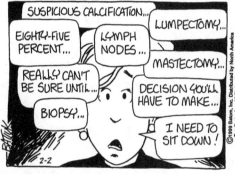

SUSPICIOUS CALCIFICATION...

EIGHTY-FIVE PERCENT...

LYMPH NODES...

LUMPECTOMY...

MASTECTOMY...

REALLY CAN'T BE SURE UNTIL...

BIOPSY...

DECISION YOU'LL HAVE TO MAKE...

I NEED TO SIT DOWN!

2-2

HONEY, YOU ARE SITTING DOWN!

THEN WHY WON'T THE ROOM STOP SPINNING?

"As a breast cancer survivor of one-and-a-half years now, you certainly are telling it like it is."

■ 9

"You have handled the subject matter in a delicate and professional manner, and I am sure you will continue to do so. You really have done a service to all women in your timely presentation."

I'VE GOT TO CONCENTRATE AND FOCUS ON THE THINGS I NEED TO DO...

2-4

NOTIFYING MY PROFS AT THE COLLEGE ... A LIST OF THINGS WE HAVE TO PICK UP... ANYTHING TO DISTRACT MYSELF FROM THINKING THE WORST!

I'VE GOT MY CANCER ALL PACKED FOR THE HOSPITAL!

THE TISSUE REMOVED FROM THE TUMOR WAS DETERMINED TO BE MALIGNANT...

2-5

WE'LL KNOW MORE AFTER WE GET THE RESULTS OF THE ESTROGEN RECEPTOR ASSAY, BUT I'M GUESSING IT'S A STAGE ONE CANCER ... AND, SINCE YOU'RE YOUNG AND HEALTHY, I'D SAY THAT YOUR PROGNOSIS IS EXCELLENT!

I APPRECIATE THAT... BUT, IF I WAS HEALTHY, I WOULDN'T BE HERE!

OVER THE COMING DAYS YOUR WIFE IS GOING TO NEED ALL THE SUPPORT YOU CAN GIVE HER...

RIGHT NOW SHE'S STILL PRETTY WOOZY FROM THE ANESTHETICS!

IS THERE ANY CHANCE THAT I COULD HAVE SOME?

2-6

THIS ALL SEEMS LIKE A BAD DREAM!

CAN THIS REALLY BE HAPPENING TO ME?

WHEN YOU'RE DIAGNOSED WITH SOMETHING LIKE CANCER... YOU SUDDENLY COME FACE TO FACE WITH YOUR OWN MORTALITY!

2-7

IT'S LIKE YOU'VE BEEN SHIFTED TO SOME COLD, DARK DIMENSION WHERE ONLY YOU EXIST!

BNK

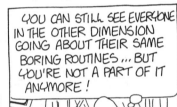

YOU CAN STILL SEE EVERYONE IN THE OTHER DIMENSION GOING ABOUT THEIR SAME BORING ROUTINES... BUT YOU'RE NOT A PART OF IT ANYMORE!

WHAT I WOULDN'T GIVE RIGHT NOW FOR THOSE SAME BORING ROUTINES!

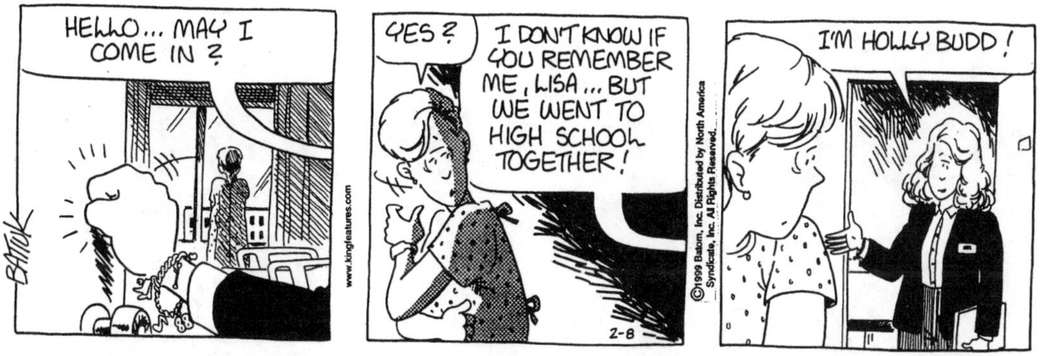
HELLO... MAY I COME IN?
BATIUK
www.kingfeatures.com
YES?
I DON'T KNOW IF YOU REMEMBER ME, LISA... BUT WE WENT TO HIGH SCHOOL TOGETHER!
2-8
©1999 Batom, Inc. Distributed by North America Syndicate, Inc. All Rights Reserved.
I'M HOLLY BUDD!

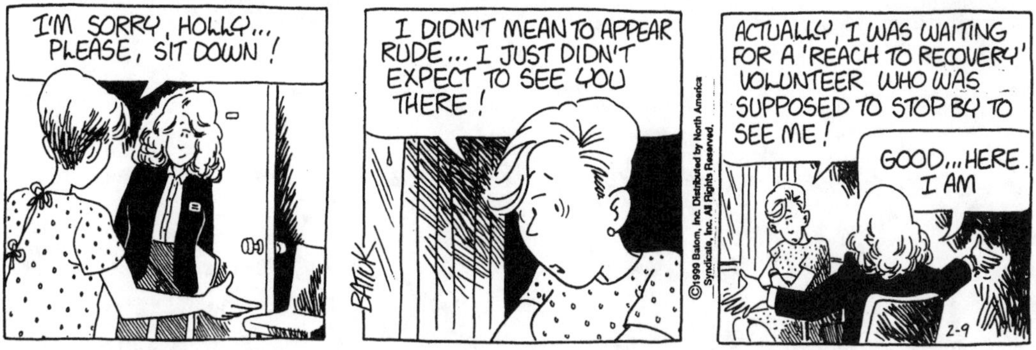
I'M SORRY, HOLLY... PLEASE, SIT DOWN!
I DIDN'T MEAN TO APPEAR RUDE... I JUST DIDN'T EXPECT TO SEE YOU THERE!
BATIUK
©1999 Batom, Inc. Distributed by North America Syndicate, Inc. All Rights Reserved.
ACTUALLY, I WAS WAITING FOR A 'REACH TO RECOVERY' VOLUNTEER WHO WAS SUPPOSED TO STOP BY TO SEE ME!
GOOD... HERE I AM
2-9

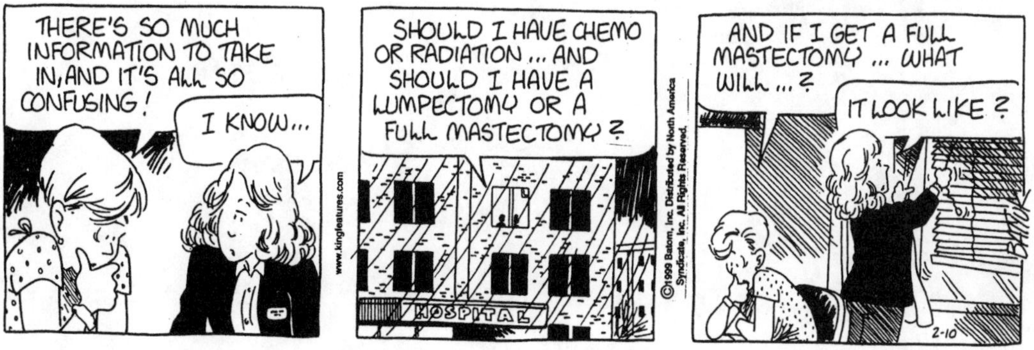
THERE'S SO MUCH INFORMATION TO TAKE IN, AND IT'S ALL SO CONFUSING!
I KNOW...
www.kingfeatures.com
SHOULD I HAVE CHEMO OR RADIATION... AND SHOULD I HAVE A LUMPECTOMY OR A FULL MASTECTOMY?
HOSPITAL
©1999 Batom, Inc. Distributed by North America Syndicate, Inc. All Rights Reserved.
AND IF I GET A FULL MASTECTOMY... WHAT WILL...?
IT LOOK LIKE?
2-10

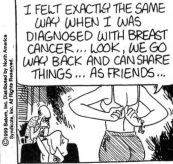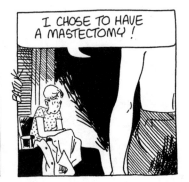

"*I was diagnosed with breast cancer in September 1998 and* Lisa's Story *could not be any closer to what happened in my life . . . So it really helps to have a good laugh at this whole saga.*"

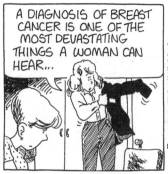

A DIAGNOSIS OF BREAST CANCER IS ONE OF THE MOST DEVASTATING THINGS A WOMAN CAN HEAR...

BUT I MADE IT THROUGH THE OPERATION AND THE CHEMO AND I'M STILL HERE TO TELL THE STORY!

HOW LONG...?

2-12

IT'S BEEN FIVE YEARS, NINE MONTHS AND TWO DAYS ... BUT WHO'S COUNTING?

EVEN IF EVERYTHING I HAVE TO GO THROUGH IS SUCCESSFUL ... THERE WILL ALWAYS BE THAT FEAR THAT MAYBE ONE DAY...

2-13

THAT'S SOMETHING WE ALL HAVE TO DEAL WITH IN OUR OWN WAY, LISA ... BUT I'VE FOUND THAT IF YOU PUT ONE FOOT IN FRONT OF THE OTHER AND JUST KEEP GOING ...

HOSPITAL

YOU CAN'T STAY AFRAID FOR THE REST OF YOUR LIFE!

DENING
BIOGRAP
HISTORY
ORTS
FICTION
WOMEN'S HEALTH
New
ISAAC ASIMOV
OH, I FORGOT... THERE'S ONE MORE THING I WANTED TO GET!
www.kingfeatures.com
READ
TO MY VALENTINE
THE BREAST CANCER GUIDE
BATIUK
©1999 Batom, Inc. Distributed by North America Syndicate, Inc. All Rights Reserved.
BOOK STORE
2·14

I PICKED UP SEVERAL BOOKS ON BREAST CANCER AT THE BOOKSTORE SO WE CAN DO SOME RESEARCH AND STUDY YOUR OPTIONS!

WHY DON'T YOU JUST LIE DOWN AND TAKE IT EASY WHILE I GO OUT AND TRY TO SCARE UP SOME SUPPER!

2-15

WE REALLY APPRECIATE ALL OF THIS!

IF THERE'S ANYTHING ELSE THAT YOU GUYS NEED, JUST HOLLER!

I DIDN'T HAVE ANY FOOD TO BRING, SO I WASHED YOUR CAR!

MONTONI'S PIZZA

2-16

MAY I HELP YOU?

YES... I CAN'T SEEM TO ACCESS THE INFORMATION I NEED ON THE INTERNET!

WESTVIEW PUBLIC LIBRARY

2-17

WHAT SUBJECT ARE YOU TRYING TO RESEARCH?

BREAST CANCER!

OH, YES... OUR BLOCKING SOFTWARE WILL KICK THAT WORD RIGHT OUT OF THERE!

"You are hitting my 'nerve' with your breast cancer story... Thanks for trying to 'educate' in your work... and keep it up, please."

Three days later

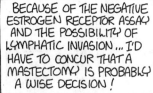

"Having been diagnosed with breast cancer, I really appreciate the treatment of the subject in this story. . . . The fear and uncertainty is so well expressed."

BATIUK
2-21
ARE YOU OKAY?
UH-HUH...
www.kingfeatures.com
I WISH I COULD HELP...
©1999 Batom, Inc. Distributed by North America Syndicate, Inc. All Rights Reserved.
BUT I CAN'T BE STRONG ENOUGH FOR BOTH OF US!

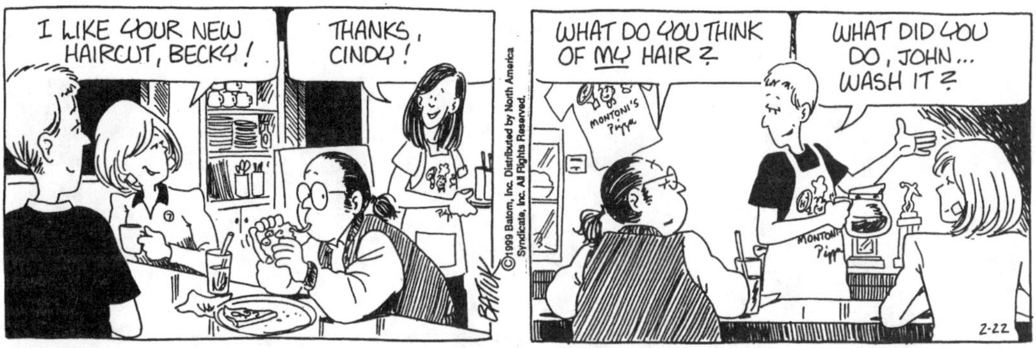
I LIKE YOUR NEW HAIRCUT, BECKY!
THANKS, CINDY!
WHAT DO YOU THINK OF MY HAIR?
WHAT DID YOU DO, JOHN... WASH IT?
MONTONI'S Pizza
BATIUK
2-22
©1999 Batom, Inc. Distributed by North America Syndicate, Inc. All Rights Reserved.

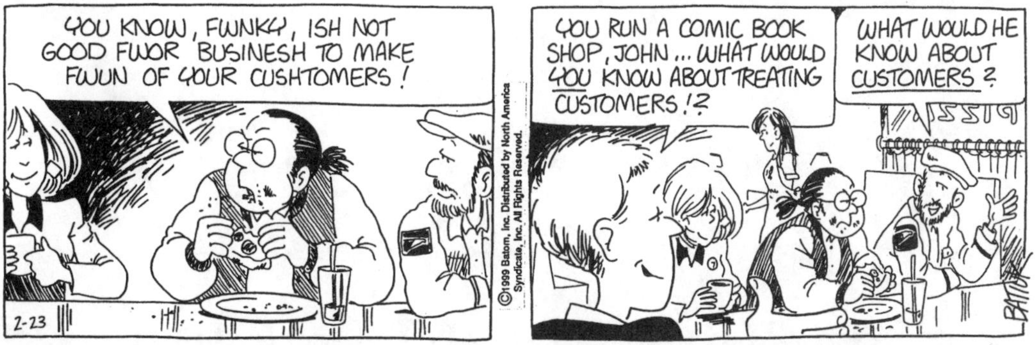
YOU KNOW, FUNKY, ISH NOT GOOD FWOR BUSINESH TO MAKE FWUN OF YOUR CUSHTOMERS!
YOU RUN A COMIC BOOK SHOP, JOHN... WHAT WOULD YOU KNOW ABOUT TREATING CUSTOMERS!?
WHAT WOULD HE KNOW ABOUT CUSTOMERS?
2-23
BATIUK
©1999 Batom, Inc. Distributed by North America Syndicate, Inc. All Rights Reserved.

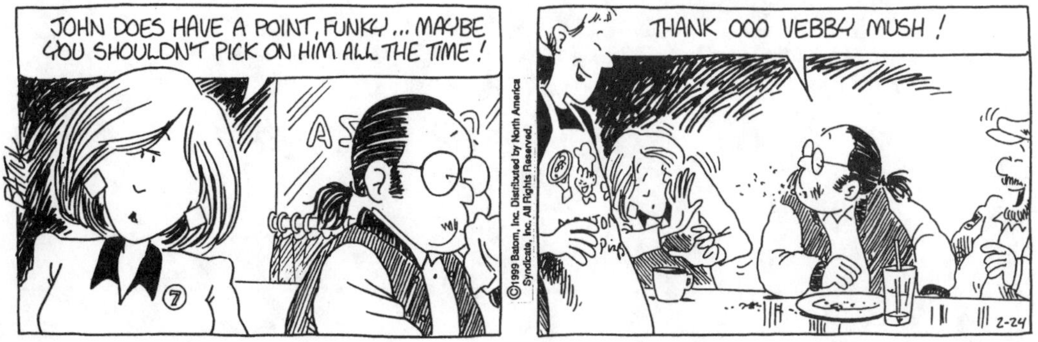
JOHN DOES HAVE A POINT, FUNKY... MAYBE YOU SHOULDN'T PICK ON HIM ALL THE TIME!
THANK OOO VEBBY MUSH!
2-24
©1999 Batom, Inc. Distributed by North America Syndicate, Inc. All Rights Reserved.

*"Our whole family enjoys Lisa's Story . . .
You are showing this whole process in such a
clear, yet true manner. You are dealing with
everything so tastefully yet truthfully, no
hiding the reality of it all."*

"I am a breast cancer survivor who wants you to know just how accurate and insightful Lisa's Story is."

Two weeks later

I JUST THOUGHT I'D COME UP TO SEE IF THERE WAS ANYTHING I COULD DO TO HELP!

NOT UNLESS YOU'VE DISCOVERED A CURE FOR CANCER!

WELL, NOW THAT YOU'VE POINTED OUT THE ELEPHANT IN THE ROOM, LISA... HOW ARE YOU FEELING?

ACTUALLY, IF I HADN'T BEEN TOLD THAT I HAVE CANCER, I'D NEVER KNOW IT... I FEEL FINE!

THERE YOU GO, LISA... THAT'S A GREAT SIGN THAT YOU'RE GOING TO BEAT THIS THING!

MONTONI'S Pizza

BATIUK

YOU KNOW, THEY GAVE ME SOME PILLS TO HELP CALM ME DOWN... BUT WHAT REALLY HELPS IS HAVING GOOD FRIENDS LIKE YOU, FUNKY!

FRIENDSHIP, SCHMENDSHIP... THIS IS STRICTLY BUSINESS! I'M JUST MAKING SURE THAT NOTHING HAPPENS TO MY BEST WAITRESS!

3-21

I'VE GOT EVERYTHING IN THE CAR!

WE'D BETTER GET GOING IF WE'RE GOING TO GET TO THE HOSPITAL BY SIX-THIRTY!

ARE YOU READY?

NO...

IF THEY HAD WANTED US AT THE HOSPITAL ANY EARLIER, THEY COULD'VE JUST SAVED ON THE ANESTHESIA BY LETTING ME SLEEP THROUGH THE OPERATION!

THAT'S PROBABLY WHAT OUR HMO WAS HOPING FOR!

"*Lisa's Story* should not be viewed as a scare tactic, but as a wake-up call even though Lisa wasn't 'sick.' As a doctor once told me, there are only two things you need to have to get breast cancer and those are breasts."

TOMORROW ON JERRY SPRINGER... BIGAMISTS WHO CHEAT ON BOTH OF THEIR WIVES!

WHY DO THEY HAVE THIS STUFF BLARING IN EVERY WAITING AREA?

IT'S THE DRUG COMPANIES' IDEA!

3-25

WE'RE BACK, AND I'D LIKE TO REMIND THE AUDIENCE NOT TO THROW THINGS AT THE GUESTS!

IT HELPS SELL MORE ANTIDEPRESSANTS!

I DON'T KNOW WHY THEY HAD US SHOW UP HERE AT THE HOSPITAL SO EARLY!

3-26

WE'VE BEEN WAITING HERE FOR OVER AN HOUR AND A HALF!

WE'RE READY FOR YOU, MRS. MOORE!

SO SOON?

IT LOOKS LIKE YOU BENT THOSE PRETTY GOOD!

YEAH... I WAS KISSING MY WIFE GOODBYE AS THEY WHEELED HER INTO THE ELEVATOR AND THE DOORS CLOSED ON MY HEAD!

THERE...FIXED! NOW ALL I HAVE TO DO IS HOPE THAT THE RINGING IN MY EARS STOPS SOON!

3-27

27

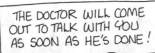

EXCUSE ME ... BUT IT SEEMS LIKE MY WIFE HAS BEEN IN THERE AN AWFULLY LONG TIME !

THE DOCTOR WILL COME OUT TO TALK WITH YOU AS SOON AS HE'S DONE !

SHE'S GOING TO BE **OKAY !!**

3-28

"*Lisa's Story* is just such an excellent tool to use to help others."

"*Once again I just want to thank you for dealing with an issue that some may feel is taboo for the funnies.*"

"Through humor and awareness we can conquer many of life's obstacles. Thank you for having the courage and foresight to take on this one."

The next week

FEEL UP TO A LITTLE FRESH AIR, HONEY?
YOU KNOW... MAYBE A WALK WOULD BE GOOD FOR ME!
www.kingfeatures.com
©1999 Batom, Inc. Distributed by North America Syndicate, Inc. All Rights Reserved.
4-4
I FEEL LIKE WALKING... BUT MY BODY FEELS LIKE RUNNING AND HIDING!

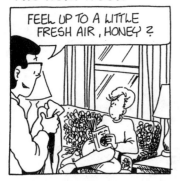

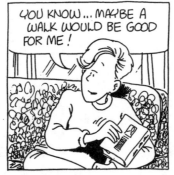

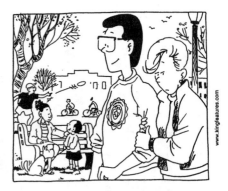

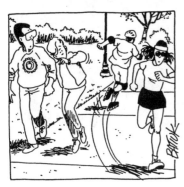

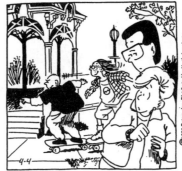

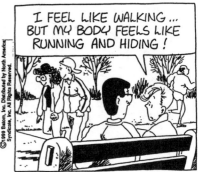

One week after surgery

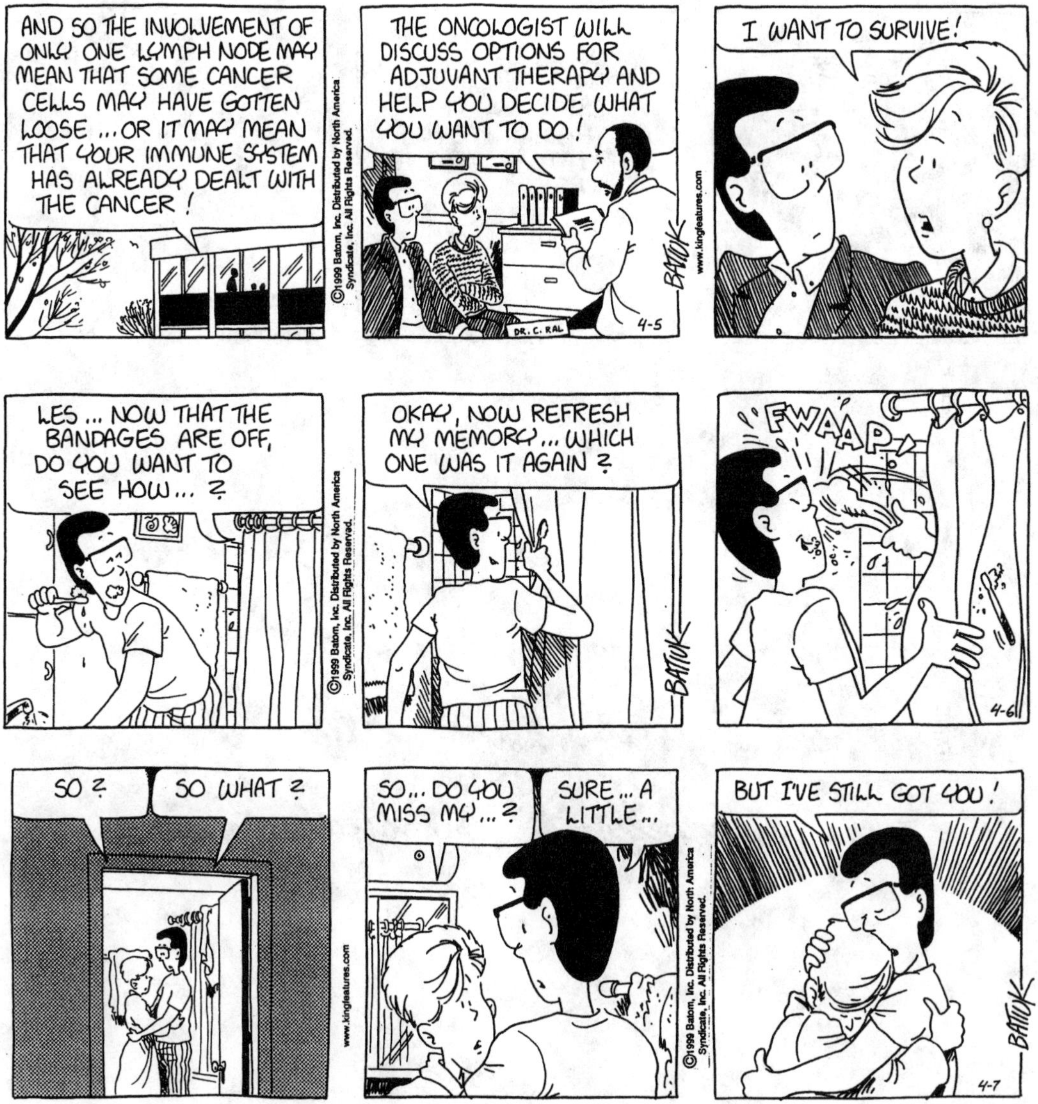
AND SO THE INVOLVEMENT OF ONLY ONE LYMPH NODE MAY MEAN THAT SOME CANCER CELLS MAY HAVE GOTTEN LOOSE ... OR IT MAY MEAN THAT YOUR IMMUNE SYSTEM HAS ALREADY DEALT WITH THE CANCER !
THE ONCOLOGIST WILL DISCUSS OPTIONS FOR ADJUVANT THERAPY AND HELP YOU DECIDE WHAT YOU WANT TO DO !
DR. C. RAL
I WANT TO SURVIVE!
LES ... NOW THAT THE BANDAGES ARE OFF, DO YOU WANT TO SEE HOW ... ?
OKAY, NOW REFRESH MY MEMORY ... WHICH ONE WAS IT AGAIN ?
FWAAP
SO ?
SO WHAT ?
SO ... DO YOU MISS MY ... ?
SURE ... A LITTLE ...
BUT I'VE STILL GOT YOU !
©1999 Batom, Inc. Distributed by North America Syndicate, Inc. All Rights Reserved.
www.kingfeatures.com

"You have done a great service by providing women with a story that deals with important health issues, and furthermore, it is an excellent topic of discussion among coworkers."

"My husband and I have shared smiles and tears after reading Lisa's Story."

Two weeks later

IT LOOKS LIKE DR. HALLETT'S OFFICE IS ON THE FOURTH FLOOR!

IT'S AMAZING HOW MY LIFE HAS CHANGED!

LAST YEAR AT THIS TIME, I COULDN'T EVEN SPELL THE WORD ONCOLOGIST!

4-26

YOU'LL BE ON A CHEMOTHERAPY PROTOCOL KNOWN AS CMF... WHICH CONTAINS THE DRUGS CYTOXAN, METHOTREXATE AND 5-FLUOROURACIL!

IT WILL CONSIST OF TWO WEEKS ON THE DRUGS FOLLOWED BY TWO WEEKS OFF... FOR A PERIOD OF SIX MONTHS!

4-27

WOW... IT LOOKS LIKE I'M REALLY GOING TO HAVE A REASON TO CELEBRATE COLUMBUS DAY THIS YEAR!

DO YOU HAVE ANY CHILDREN?

NO... WHY?

I WAS JUST GOING TO SAY THAT IF YOU'VE EVER BEEN PREGNANT... YOU'D FIND THAT CHEMO IS A LOT LIKE MORNING SICKNESS!

DR. LESLIE HALLETT — ONCOLOGIST

4-28

ACTUALLY... I HAVE HAD SOME EXPERIENCE WITH THAT!

I WAS THINKING ABOUT WHAT DR. HALLETT SAID ABOUT LISTENING TO SOOTHING MUSIC WHILE YOU'RE RECEIVING THE CHEMOTHERAPY... SO I MADE YOU THIS TAPE!

'MUSIC FOR INJECTING POISONOUS CHEMICALS'... CATCHY!

ACTUALLY, I WAS THINKING OF CALLING IT 'WOODSTOCK III', BUT...

HOW IS LISA DOING WITH THE CHEMOTHERAPY?

WELL, I MADE DINNER FOR HER AFTER HER FIRST SESSION, AND SHE TOOK ONE LOOK AT IT AND THREW UP!

I REMEMBER DOING THAT WHEN WE ROOMED TOGETHER AND YOU COOKED DINNER!

TRUE...

THE WORST THING ABOUT THE CHEMOTHERAPY IS THIS CONSTANT QUEASY FEELING!

I KNOW WHAT YOU NEED TO DO... COME WITH ME!

GRANDMA... LISA NEEDS YOUR HELP!

GRANDMA'S KNOWLEDGE OF HERB HEALING COMES FROM FAMILY SECRETS THAT HAVE BEEN PASSED DOWN THROUGH THE AGES!

SHE CAN HELP YOU WITH THE SICKNESS FROM THE CHEMOTHERAPY AS WELL AS RESTORE YOUR BODY'S NATURAL CHI!

PLEASE SIT!

WE MUST ADDRESS THE IMBALANCE IN YOUR BODY... SO THAT YOUR BODY MAY REGAIN ITS NATURAL STATE!

YOU CAN TELL THIS BY TAKING MY PULSE?

NO... BY LISTENING TO YOUR PULSE!

DOCTORS TALK TO YOU ABOUT YOUR BODY...

BUT WITH GRANDMOTHER... YOUR BODY TALKS TO HER!

5-2

"You are really performing a public service by bringing breast cancer and early detection of it to the forefront."

LIU LIN'S GRANDMOTHER SAID TO BOIL THESE HERBS AND THEN DRINK THE CONCOCTION TO RESTORE MY BODY'S NATURAL BALANCE!

SHE MUST KNOW SOMETHING ... SHE SMOKES LIKE A CHIMNEY, AND IS THE PICTURE OF HEALTH! NEITHER YOU NOR I SMOKE, AND WE BOTH ENDED UP WITH CANCER!

AND THEY SAY THE FATES HAVE NO SENSE OF HUMOR!

5-5

IT LOOKS LIKE MY BABE IS FEELING BETTER ... SHE'S STARTED SUPPER!

HI, HONEY ...THOSE HERBS I GOT FROM LIN'S GRANDMOTHER ...

REALLY SEEM TO HELP WITH MY NAUSEA!

5-6

ARE YOU SURE YOU'RE REALLY UP TO THIS, LISA?

COMMUNI
COLLE

DON'T WORRY ... WHEN I GET HOME FROM CLASS, I'LL TAKE A LONG NAP!

5-7

HEY ... DON'T FORGET YOUR SLIME SOUP!

OH ... MY HERB WATER!

"Thank you for handling such a sensitive matter in an enlightened and straightforward manner."

Four weeks after beginning chemotherapy

42 ∎

LOOK... IF YOU'RE NOT IN THE MOOD, LISA, THAT'S OKAY!

5-27

DR. HALLETT SAID THAT IT WAS IMPORTANT FOR YOU TO LISTEN TO YOUR BODY!

RIGHT NOW... YOU DON'T WANT TO HEAR THE LANGUAGE MY BODY IS USING!

HOW ABOUT IF YOU FIX YOURSELF SOMETHING TO EAT... I'M GOING TO LIE DOWN!

5-28

THAT'S GOOD... DR. HALLETT SAID THAT THE BEST THING FOR YOU WAS TO DRINK PLENTY OF FLUIDS AND REST!

I'VE GOT NEWS FOR YOU... THEY'RE MUTUALLY EXCLUSIVE!

"On behalf of women everywhere I thank you for exploring this topic in a way that only you will be able to do."

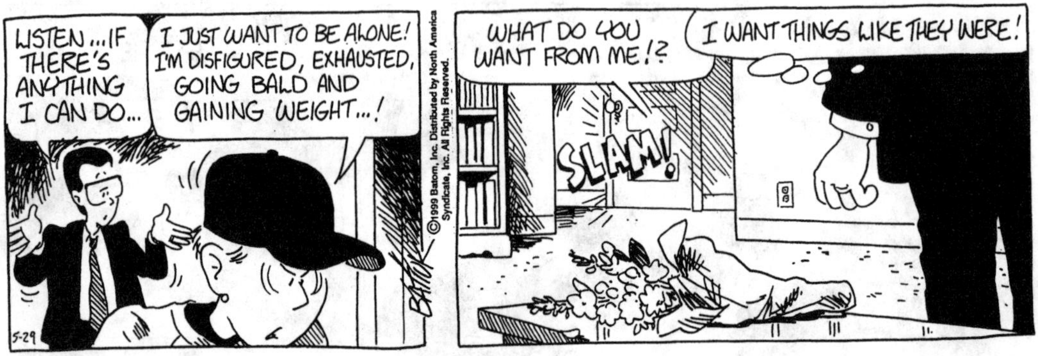
LISTEN ...IF THERE'S ANYTHING I CAN DO...
I JUST WANT TO BE ALONE! I'M DISFIGURED, EXHAUSTED, GOING BALD AND GAINING WEIGHT...!
5-29
BATIUK
©1999 Batom, Inc. Distributed by North America Syndicate, Inc. All Rights Reserved.
WHAT DO YOU WANT FROM ME!?
SLAM!
I WANT THINGS LIKE THEY WERE!

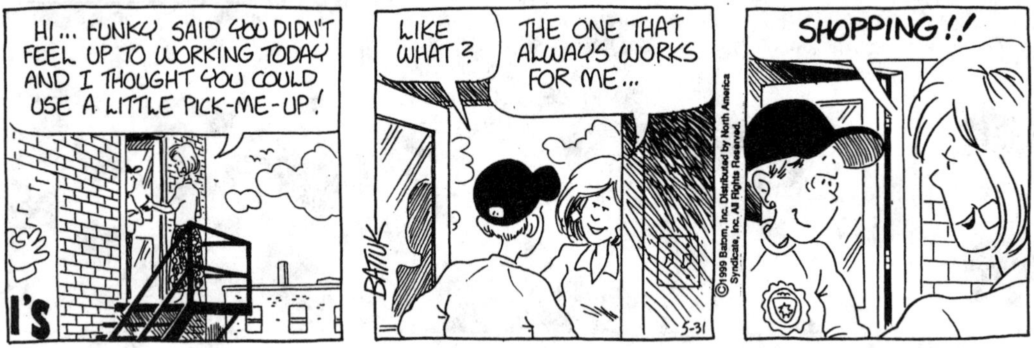
HI ... FUNKY SAID YOU DIDN'T FEEL UP TO WORKING TODAY AND I THOUGHT YOU COULD USE A LITTLE PICK-ME-UP!
BATIUK
LIKE WHAT ?
THE ONE THAT ALWAYS WORKS FOR ME...
5-31
©1999 Batom, Inc. Distributed by North America Syndicate, Inc. All Rights Reserved.
SHOPPING!!

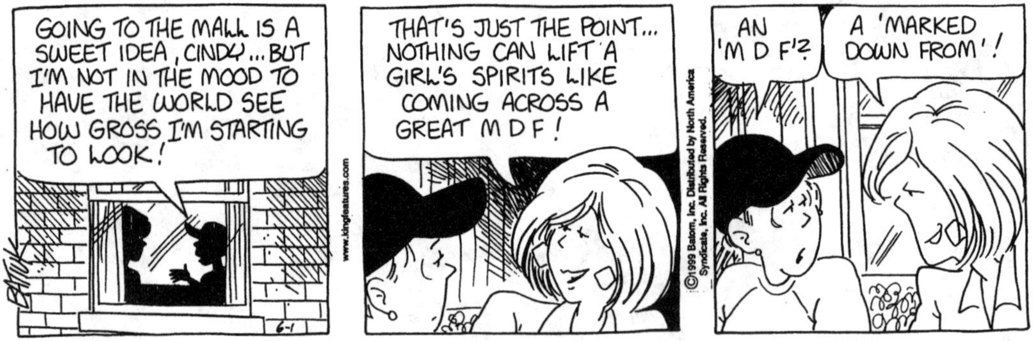
GOING TO THE MALL IS A SWEET IDEA, CINDY... BUT I'M NOT IN THE MOOD TO HAVE THE WORLD SEE HOW GROSS I'M STARTING TO LOOK!
6-1
www.kingfeatures.com
THAT'S JUST THE POINT... NOTHING CAN LIFT A GIRL'S SPIRITS LIKE COMING ACROSS A GREAT M D F!
©1999 Batom, Inc. Distributed by North America Syndicate, Inc. All Rights Reserved.
AN 'M D F'?
A 'MARKED DOWN FROM'!

"Your readers are well served by this low-key, educational approach to breast disease."

I DON'T THINK SO...

THERE'S ONLY ROOM FOR ONE BLONDE BOMBER IN THIS TOWN!

WHAT DO YOU THINK?

YOU LOOK STUNNING!

HOW'S LISA DOING, LES?

SHE'S GOING THROUGH KIND OF A TOUGH TIME WITH HER CHEMO, NATE... EACH TIME I GO HOME THESE DAYS...

'I NEVER KNOW WHAT TO EXPECT!'

"I am so sure that you will have a powerful impact on many people, not only women, but to many people who have loved ones who are women."

"You give us all a dose of hope, that no matter what it takes, this woman wants to live simply because life is so precious."

YOU MEAN TO TELL ME THERE AREN'T ANY MORE BASKETBALL GAMES LEFT?

I THINK OUR CONSTITUTIONAL RIGHTS TO WATCH A BASKETBALL GAME ARE BEING VIOLATED!

IF YOU'RE LOOKING FOR SOMETHING TO DO... YOU COULD ALWAYS SNUGGLE WITH YOUR WIFE!

AN EXCELLENT IDEA!

6-13

I LOVE YOUR HAIR, BY THE WAY... WHERE DO YOU HAVE IT DONE?

HONG KONG!

One year later

WHILE I'M ON SPRING BREAK FROM SCHOOL ... I THOUGHT THAT MAYBE I COULD HELP YOU WADE THROUGH SOME OF THE REMAINING INSURANCE PAPERWORK FROM MY BREAST CANCER TREATMENTS!

GREAT! IT'S ALL CAREFULLY FILED AWAY IN THIS MANILA FOLDER...

4-17

AND THIS MANILA FOLDER ... AND THIS MANILA FOLDER...

ARE ALL OF THESE FOLDERS FILLED WITH HOSPITAL BILLS?

NOT EXACTLY...

THIS ONE IS FOR STATEMENTS ... THIS ONE IS FOR INVOICES ... THIS THIN ONE IS FOR BILLS THAT WERE PAID BY OUR HEALTH PLAN, DENIALCARE...

4-18

AND THIS ONE IS FOR THE ONES THAT I COULDN'T FIGURE OUT!

FIRST THE HOSPITAL SENDS US A BILL TELLING US WHAT DENIALCARE HAS PAID AND WHAT WE HAVE TO PAY!

AFTER WE'VE PAID THAT... THEY SEND US A BILL FOR THE AMOUNT THAT THEY SAID DENIALCARE HAD PAID!

4-19

AND THEN A FEW MONTHS AFTER THAT, THEY SEND US A BILL FOR THE ENTIRE AMOUNT!

"Thank you for giving us breast cancer in all its rawness. You proved that not even cancer can impair the funny bone. Seeing Lisa bald is a great triumph for all of us who have suffered follicle fallout."

"*This story will help by increasing awareness of the need for early detection, that young women can get breast cancer, that it can be survived, that real men don't care about the scars or missing parts.*"

"It is a real treat to see that you have such a unique vision to share with readers the challenges of breast cancer in your creative medium."

WA...

HOO!!

I FINALLY FIGURED OUT THIS MAZE OF HOSPITAL BILLING FORMS!

ALL THAT'S LEFT IS THIS LETTER THAT CAME TODAY FROM THE HOSPITAL!

'DEAR PATIENT... WE WANT TO INFORM YOU THAT WE'RE CONVERTING TO A NEW BILLING SYSTEM...'

4-23

AAUUUUUUGGGHH!!

HOW IS LISA DOING THESE DAYS, LES? SHE'S DOING GREAT!

I THINK SHE'S FINALLY REACHED A POINT WHERE SHE'S MANAGED TO PUT ALL THOUGHTS OF CANCER BEHIND HER!

AND IT'S LIKE I LIVE MY LIFE THESE DAYS WAITING FOR THE OTHER SHOE TO DROP!

EVERY MORNING WHEN I STEP OUT OF THE SHOWER AND LOOK IN THE MIRROR... I'M REMINDED OF THE CANCER!

AND YOU WANT TO KNOW WHEN YOU CAN FINALLY GO BACK TO A HAPPILY UNAWARE EXISTENCE! EXACTLY!

YOU CAN'T!

ARE YOU OKAY?

"I found Lisa's Story to be accurate, filled with feeling, and very realistic."

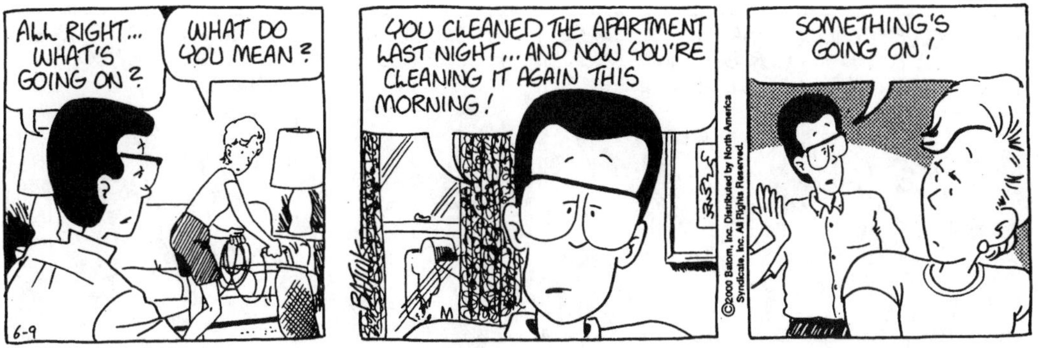
ALL RIGHT... WHAT'S GOING ON ?
WHAT DO YOU MEAN ?
YOU CLEANED THE APARTMENT LAST NIGHT... AND NOW YOU'RE CLEANING IT AGAIN THIS MORNING !
SOMETHING'S GOING ON !
BATIUK
©2000 Batom, Inc. Distributed by North America Syndicate, Inc. All Rights Reserved.
6-9

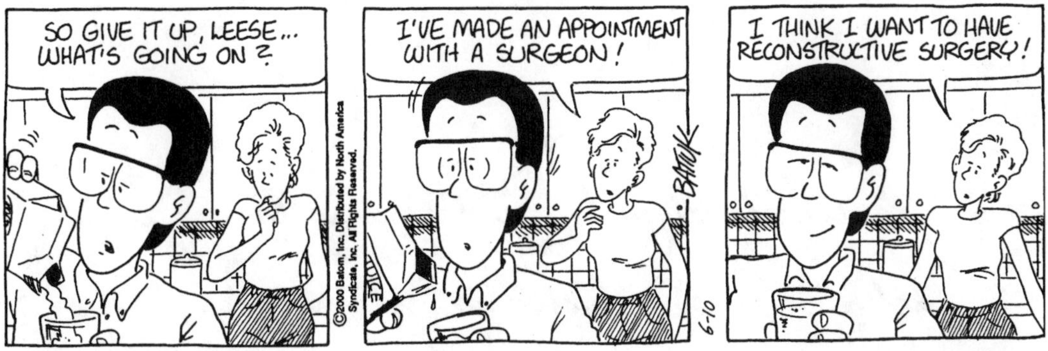
SO GIVE IT UP, LEESE... WHAT'S GOING ON ?
I'VE MADE AN APPOINTMENT WITH A SURGEON !
I THINK I WANT TO HAVE RECONSTRUCTIVE SURGERY !
©2000 Batom, Inc. Distributed by North America Syndicate, Inc. All Rights Reserved.
BATIUK
6-10

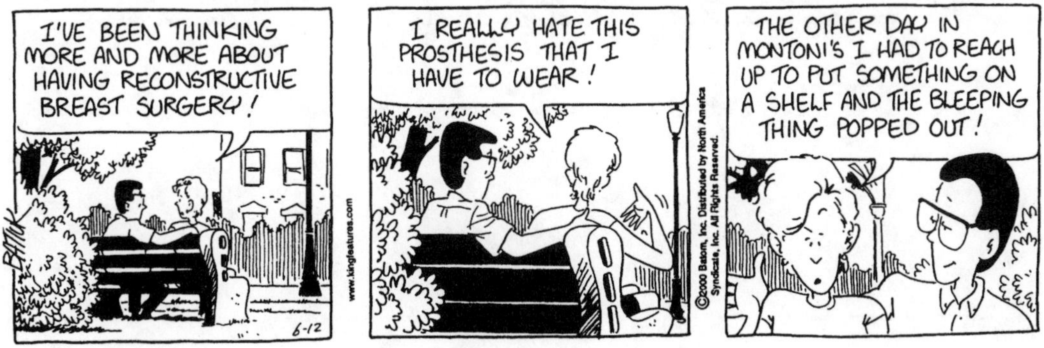
I'VE BEEN THINKING MORE AND MORE ABOUT HAVING RECONSTRUCTIVE BREAST SURGERY !
I REALLY HATE THIS PROSTHESIS THAT I HAVE TO WEAR !
THE OTHER DAY IN MONTONI'S I HAD TO REACH UP TO PUT SOMETHING ON A SHELF AND THE BLEEPING THING POPPED OUT !
BATIUK
6-12
www.kingfeatures.com
©2000 Batom, Inc. Distributed by North America Syndicate, Inc. All Rights Reserved.

"*I particularly admired the willingness to tackle serious, difficult situations and handle them with sensitivity and appropriate humor.*"

THE WOMEN'S HEALTH AND CANCER RIGHTS ACT REQUIRES THAT INSURANCE COMPANIES PAY FOR BREAST RECONSTRUCTION!

SO EVEN OUR HMO, DENIALCARE, WOULD HAVE TO PAY FOR IT!

JUST REMEMBER... YOU DON'T HAVE TO DO IT FOR ME!

I KNOW... I WANT TO DO IT FOR ME!

NOW WHEN IT COMES TO IMPLANTS ...SMALL-BREASTED WOMEN SUCH AS YOURSELF DO QUITE WELL...

IT'S JUST ONE HUMILIATION AFTER ANOTHER...

DR. HOLLMAN PLASTIC SURGERY

ALTHOUGH WE CAN ALSO RECONSTRUCT THE BREAST WITH TISSUE FROM THE ABDOMEN, BACK OR BUTTOCK AREA!

ALTHOUGH, WHAT'S ONE MORE POUND ON AN ELEPHANT?

I WANT YOU TO LOOK AT SOME PICTURES AND DISCUSS IMPLANT SIZES ...BUT FIRST I WANT TO TAKE SOME MEASUREMENTS!

I'D SAY YOU'RE ABOUT A 34 A ...?

ON A GOOD DAY!

SAY, THOSE ARE NICE!

TRY NOT TO ENJOY THIS SO MUCH!

6-17

SORRY... I GUESS I WAS JUST FLASHING BACK TO MY COLLEGE DORM-ROOM DAYS!

OUR HMO, DENIALCARE, HAS AGREED TO PAY FOR MY RECONSTRUCTIVE SURGERY... SO WHY AREN'T I HAPPY ABOUT IT?

6-19

I KNEW THAT YOU CAN EXPERIENCE A LETDOWN AFTER CHEMO IS OVER...

BUT I FIGURED THAT EVENTUALLY I'D BE LET BACK UP!

I NEVER DREAMED THAT MY LIFE WOULD TURN OUT LIKE THIS!

6-20

I GUESS THAT'S THE PROBLEM WITH DREAMS... THEY NEVER INCLUDE COMPLICATIONS...

AND A LIFE WITHOUT COMPLICATIONS JUST DOESN'T EXIST!

NO MATTER HOW GOOD THE RECONSTRUCTIVE SURGERY IS ... THINGS WILL NEVER BE THE SAME!

I'D ALWAYS PICTURED MYSELF HAVING CHILDREN AND NURSING THEM...

WEST-VIEW PARK

HOW DO YOU EXPLAIN TO A BABY THAT THE OTHER ONE IS JUST FOR SHOW?

6-21

I NEVER HAD A MODEL'S FIGURE ... BUT I ALWAYS LIKED MY BODY AND FELT GOOD ABOUT HOW I LOOKED!

WESTVIEW PARK

6-22

WHAT IS IT ABOUT GOD THAT MAKES HIM HATE PRIDE SO MUCH...

WHILE BEING SO INDIFFERENT TO SUFFERING?

MAYBE IT'S TIME FOR ME TO REALIZE THAT I CAN'T CONTROL EVERYTHING THAT'S GOING TO HAPPEN...

AND THAT THE BEST THING TO DO IS THROW THE SCRIPT AWAY...

6-23

AND JUST LET THE PLAY UNFOLD!

Panel 1:
HEY, KID... WHAT HAVE YOU BEEN UP TO ?

OH, JUST OUT WALKING AND LEARNING ABOUT LIFE !

6-24

www.kingfeatures.com

Panel 2:
AND YOU LEARNED...?

THAT LIFE ISN'T A WALK IN THE PARK...

Panel 3:
BUT THAT FACT SHOULDN'T KEEP YOU FROM ENJOYING A WALK IN THE PARK !

BATIUK

"The comic strip form may be the only way some people are exposed to very important messages, but it has a special touch even if one is well-read."

WHAT MADE YOU DECIDE TO GO INTO PLASTIC SURGERY?

6-26

I LIKE KNOWING THAT MY PATIENTS WILL BE AROUND TO ENJOY MY WORK!

YOUR WIFE CAME THROUGH THE SURGERY JUST FINE AND SHE'S RESTING COMFORTABLY!

6-27

UHHHHH....

I CAN'T BELIEVE THEY'RE SENDING ME HOME IN THIS CONDITION!

DENIALCARE, OUR HMO, WILL ONLY PAY FOR YOU TO STAY IN THE HOSPITAL ONE DAY!

IF I'M NOT SICK ENOUGH TO BE IN A HOSPITAL... I WONDER WHO IS?

6-28

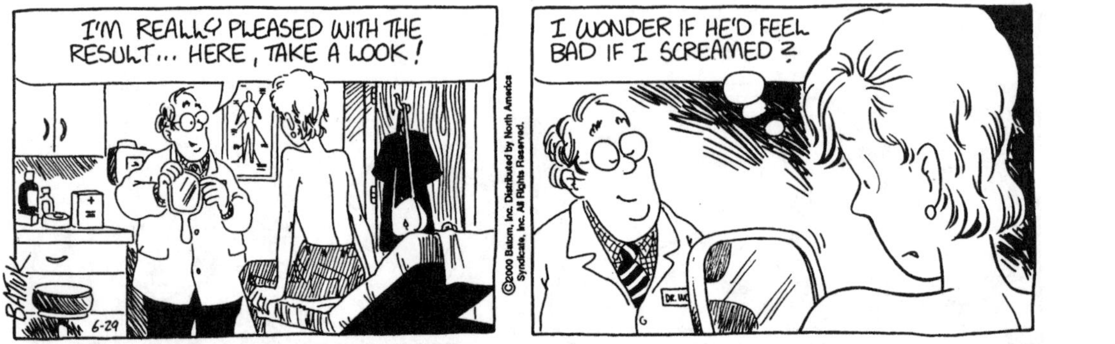
I'M REALLY PLEASED WITH THE RESULT... HERE, TAKE A LOOK!
BATIUK
6-29
©2000 Batom, Inc. Distributed by North America Syndicate, Inc. All Rights Reserved.
I WONDER IF HE'D FEEL BAD IF I SCREAMED?

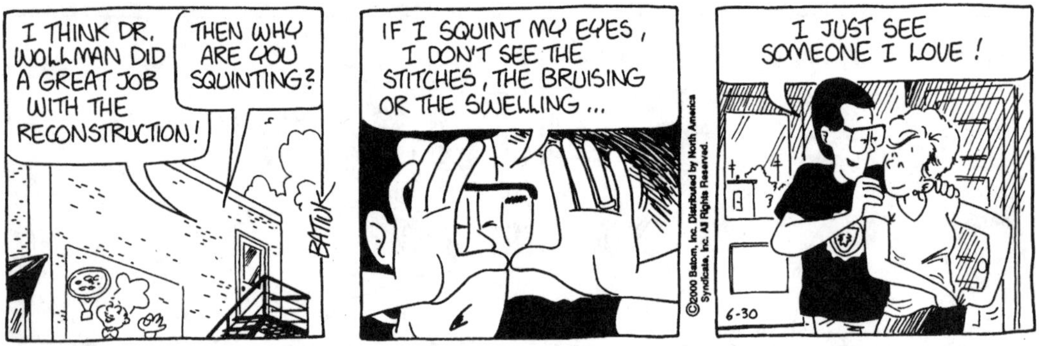
I THINK DR. WOLLMAN DID A GREAT JOB WITH THE RECONSTRUCTION!
THEN WHY ARE YOU SQUINTING?
BATIUK
IF I SQUINT MY EYES, I DON'T SEE THE STITCHES, THE BRUISING OR THE SWELLING...
©2000 Batom, Inc. Distributed by North America Syndicate, Inc. All Rights Reserved.
I JUST SEE SOMEONE I LOVE!
6-30

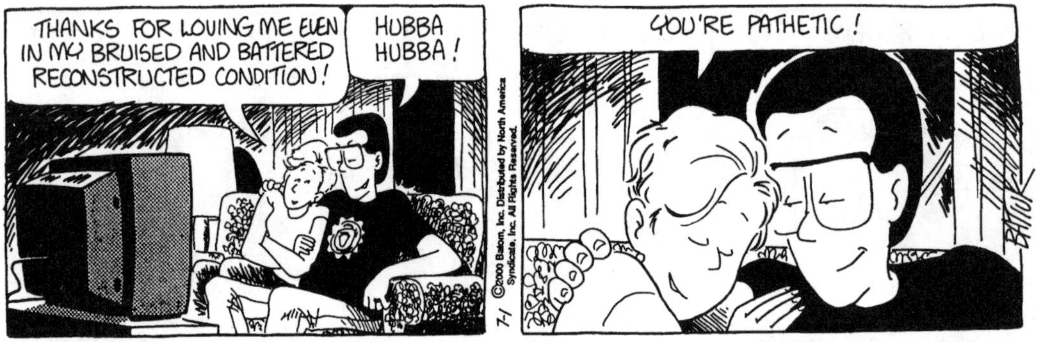
THANKS FOR LOVING ME EVEN IN MY BRUISED AND BATTERED RECONSTRUCTED CONDITION!
HUBBA HUBBA!
7-1
©2000 Batom, Inc. Distributed by North America Syndicate, Inc. All Rights Reserved.
YOU'RE PATHETIC!
BATIUK

SO DOES LISA HAVE A CLASS TONIGHT, LES?

NO... ACTUALLY, TONIGHT'S THE NIGHT THAT HER CLUB MEETS...

I'D LIKE TO WELCOME A NEW MEMBER THIS EVENING TO OUR BREAST CANCER SUPPORT GROUP...

WHEN I WENT THROUGH CHEMO, I FOUND THERE WERE TWO THINGS I NEEDED MORE THAN ANYTHING ELSE...

WESTVIEW COMMUNITY CENTER

A LOT OF LOVE AND NAPS...

MOSTLY NAPS!

SINCE I'VE BEEN ON CHEMO... OUR FRIENDS AND RELATIVES HAVE PROVIDED MEALS ALMOST EVERY NIGHT...

AND MY HUSBAND HAS BEEN SO WONDERFUL HELPING WITH THE HOUSEWORK AND THE KIDS!

I'M ALMOST GOING TO HATE TO SEE THE CHEMO END!

I DON'T HAVE A HUSBAND OR A BOYFRIEND AT THE MOMENT... BUT I DO HAVE A CAT...

AND I'VE LEARNED THAT CATS DON'T FRET ABOUT THE PAST OR WORRY ABOUT WHAT MIGHT HAPPEN IN THE FUTURE... THEY JUST EXIST IN THE MOMENT, AND IT MADE ME REALIZE THAT TODAY IS CALLED 'THE PRESENT'...

BECAUSE IT'S A GIFT!

IF ANYONE WOULD LIKE TO MODEL WIGS AND CLOTHING IN OUR BREAST CANCER FASHION SHOW NEXT WEEK... SEE ME AT THE END OF THE MEETING!

IF THIS IS WHAT IT TAKES TO BREAK INTO MODELING... YOU CAN HAVE IT!

DON'T FORGET THAT IF YOU CAN'T MAKE IT TO OUR SUPPORT GROUP MEETING...

THERE'S A LOCAL BREAST CANCER CHAT ROOM THAT YOU CAN ACCESS ON THE INTERNET!

IS THERE AN UNBURDENING, UNLOADING, LET IT ALL HANG OUT ROOM?

Resources from NABCO (National Alliance of Breast Cancer Organizations)

*Formed in 1986, NABCO is the leading nonprofit information and education resource on breast cancer and a national force in patient advocacy. NABCO provides information to medical professionals and their organizations, patients and their families and the media. In addition, NABCO advocates for regulatory change, legislation and clinical advances that benefit patients, survivors and women at risk. With public and corporate partners, NABCO has collaborated on educational and medical programs that have been successful in reaching a national audience, heightening public awareness and connecting women with needed services. For additional information, pleases contact **NABCO, 9 East 37th Street, New York, New York 10016; (888) 80-NABCO** or **www.nabco.org**.*

1. Could This Be Breast Cancer?

You've found a breast lump, or something that seems or looks abnormal. Before you panic, think about these things:

- *Breast lumps.* They are common, and not a cause for alarm. Things to look out for are asymmetry (something that's only on one side), a change that does not go away after a few weeks or one menstrual cycle, and skin puckering or any difference in appearance. If you have any of these signs, get your breasts checked by a doctor or nurse.

- *A change since your scheduled breast exam.* If you're in your twenties, you should be having a breast exam by a medical professional every year. Once you turn forty, add a screening mammogram every year. If you have a family history of breast cancer in a close relative or a personal history of cysts or benign breast biopsies, talk to your doctor about starting mammography earlier. If you notice a change and it's been more than six months since your last breast exam, be sure to mention the date of your last exam to your doctor or nurse.

- *Other causes for breast lumps and tenderness.* Some women find that caffeine causes breast tenderness, so eliminate coffee, tea and chocolate and look for changes. Is it time for your menstrual period? (Lumps and swelling are common then.) Did you begin any new medication, including oral contraceptives or other hormonal medications?

Lisa's Story

Normal Breast Conditions

The Informed Woman's Guide to Breast Health by Kerry A. McGinn (Bull Publishing, Palo Alto, CA, 1992, paperback $13.95). A thorough overview of the detection and treatment of breast lumps and conditions that are benign (not cancer). Includes a glossary. 127 pages. **Bookstores.**

"**Understanding Breast Changes: A Health Guide for All Women**" (P051, 1998). This free booklet explains various types of breast changes that women experience and outlines methods that doctors use to distinguish between benign changes and cancer. Fifty-two pages. Call **The National Cancer Institute's Cancer Information Service, (800) 4-CANCER.**

Breast Examinations

Breast Self-Examination Shower Card (2028-LE). This free plastic shower card guides you through breast self-examination. Call the **American Cancer Society, (800) ACS-2345.**

"**How to Do Breast Self-Examination**" (2088-LE). This free pamphlet gives specific instructions on breast self-examination. Call the **ACS, (800) ACS-2345.**

Mammography

"**How to Get a Low-Cost Mammogram**" (June 1999). This free one-page NABCO fact sheet suggests ways to get a low-cost mammogram for women without insurance coverage. Contact **National Alliance of Breast Cancer Organizations (888) 80-NABCO** or **www.nabco.org.**

"Mammograms . . . Not Just Once, But for a Lifetime!" (P392, September 1997). A free two-page, easy-to-read card that defines mammography and describes who needs one, and the step-by-step procedure. Spanish language version available. Call the **NCI's CIS, (800) 4-CANCER.**

"The Older You Get, the More You Need a Mammogram" (5020.00-LE, 1996). A free pamphlet that discusses the importance of early detection as a woman ages, and some of the issues of concern to older women. Call the **ACS, (800) ACS-2345.**

GETTING THE BEST MAMMOGRAM

All women are at risk for breast cancer, and most know that the best way to treat breast cancer successfully is to find it early. A mammogram can detect breast cancer before it can be felt, yet many women wonder when to begin getting mammograms, how often, and how to know for certain that they are getting the best quality mammograms available. Here are NABCO's recommended steps for getting the best possible mammogram:

- Look for the FDA certificate, which should be prominently displayed at the facility. Facilities not meeting FDA requirements may not lawfully perform mammography.

- Know what to expect. Order and read "Things to Know About Quality Mammograms," the consumer version of the government's Agency for Health Care

Lisa's Story

Policy and Research (AHCPR) quality guidelines. Share a copy with other women you know, and ask your doctors to obtain a supply for their patients. Order this free booklet in English or Spanish by calling **(800) 358-9295.**

■ Get regular mammograms. Once is not enough. NABCO recommends that annual screening begin at age forty. In addition, schedule an annual clinical breast exam to be performed by a physician or nurse. Also, be familiar with your breasts and examine them monthly.

■ Time your mammogram well, follow instructions, and be prepared with information about your health. Schedule your mammogram when your breasts will be least tender, such as the week after your menstrual period. Wear a two-piece outfit to make undressing more convenient and avoid using deodorant and lotions that day, which can affect the film. Bringing prior mammographic films (which you have the right to receive upon request) and being prepared with your health history will help the fast and accurate interpretation of your test results.

■ Take charge of your follow-up. New FDA regulations now require mammography facilities to provide you with a report of your mammogram results. Tell the facility the name of a physician who should also receive them. If you do not have results within ten days, call the facility yourself. If follow-up exams or procedures are recommended, schedule them promptly. Rescreen each year at the same facility, or ask that your films be sent to your new provider. Make a list of questions for your doctor, and call **NABCO** at **(888) 80-NABCO** for more information.

BREAST CANCER RISK

The 1995 discovery of the BRCA1 and BRCA2 breast cancer susceptibility genes has added an important dimension to counseling women who may be at high risk of developing breast cancer as well as other diseases. Currently, a limited number of trained genetic counselors are expert in cancer susceptibility, and professionals are still investigating the types of information and interventions most helpful to women considering being tested for genetic mutations. This important information will be best obtained from testing conducted in the context of investigational protocols that protect the confidentiality of women and their families.

Some useful resources:

- **AstraZeneca Pharmaceuticals Patient Education Service** offers free patient education materials on risk reduction, breast cancer and tamoxifen therapy. Contact **AstraZeneca Pharmaceuticals, 1800 Concord Pike, Wilmington, DE 19850 (800) 34-LIFE-4** or **www.astrazeneca.com.**

- **The Family Cancer Risk Counseling and Genetic Testing Directory** offers a listing of cancer risk counseling resources and genetic testing providers across the country. This online service is found on **CancerNet™**, the web site of the National Cancer Institute (NCI), and can be accessed by visiting the web site at **cancernet.nci.nih.gov/genesrch.shtml** (no "www" is needed). This directory is searchable by name, city, state, country, and type of cancer or cancer gene.

- *NABCO News.* The quarterly *NABCO News* publishes ongoing updates on breast cancer genetic susceptibility. Join NABCO to receive the newsletter, or

Lisa's Story

page through archived issues on NABCO's web site at **www.nabco.org** to find the following *NABCO News* articles:

- "BRCA1 Mutation Identified in Ashkenazi Jews" (October 1995)

- "Genetic Susceptibility: An Update" (January 1996)

- "Controversies Emerge with BRCA1 Testing" (April 1996)

- "Genetic Testing Update" (April 1997)

- "Genetics in the Real World: Some Answers, More Questions" (July 1997)

- **Cancer centers.** Many cancer centers have developed their own materials to give women general background information on risk assessment and genetic testing, as well as details about their particular programs.

- **On the web.** Useful resources from **The Alliance of Genetic Support Groups** are at **www.geneticalliance.org.** For a list of the members of the **National Society of Genetic Counselors** who have expertise in familial cancer risk counseling and are available for referrals, e-mail **NSCC@aol.com** or call **(610) 872-7608.**

- **"Understanding Gene Testing"** (T922, 1997). This free easy-to-understand guide provides readers with basic information and addresses issues raised when considering testing under managed care. Thirty pages. Call the **NCI's CIS, (800) 4-CANCER.**

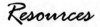

- **"Understanding Genetics of Breast Cancer for Jewish Women"** (American Jewish Congress and Hadassah, 1997). As a follow-up to the First Leadership Conference on Jewish Women's Health Issues, this brochure was compiled to answer questions about hereditary risk of breast cancer and deciding whether to undergo genetic testing. Useful for all women concerned about hereditary breast cancer. Contact **Hadassah Health Education Department, (212) 303-8094** or **www.hadassah.org.**

2. Diagnosis

Your doctor is concerned, and can't yet reassure you that your lump is *not* breast cancer. In the process of an abnormal "work up," here are the first things you'll want to think about:

- *What's the first step?* After a physical breast exam that professional will probably refer you to an imaging facility for more tests. The imaging facility will offer a range of technologies, including mammography (breast X rays) and ultrasound (using sound waves to form a picture of the breast structures). Mammography facilities are now government-certified to offer safe and accurate tests.

- *Imaging tests.* The tests given to you at the imaging facility will depend on your age, the abnormality in your breast, and the report of the physical exam by your doctor. The imaging facility's professionals will examine your breast again, and mark the area in question. If you have a mammogram, additional pictures or views might be taken to get a close-up or clearer image.

Lisa's Story

- *Needle aspiration.* If the imaging tests are inconclusive or look suggestive of breast cancer, some form of biopsy—removing cells or tissue for examination—is the next step. Although some imaging facilities can perform the next phase of tests, at this point many women will be referred to a surgical specialist. The specialist will either attempt to withdraw cells or fluid by inserting a needle in the breast—called a needle aspiration—or will recommend a biopsy as the next step.

- *Biopsy.* A biopsy is the removal of additional cells or tissue for examination under a microscope. A core needle image–guided biopsy is the newest form of this procedure. It is minimally invasive and is performed in a radiology office. Other forms of biopsy require surgery as a hospital outpatient or inpatient. The majority of breast biopsies turn out not to be breast cancer!

- *Information.* This is a good time to take advantage of the many sources for free information about breast cancer and breast exams. See below for the toll-free numbers and web sites of national and local breast cancer organizations.

General Information About Cancer and Breast Cancer

"Ask NABCO^{SM}**"** is NABCO's online column that answers common questions about risk, detection and treatment of breast cancer. Contact NABCO, **(888) 80-NABCO** or **www.nabco.org** to order a hard copy version of one or more features. To submit questions, e-mail **asknabco@aol.com.**

Books

Bosom Buddies: Lessons and Laughter on Breast Health and Cancer by Rosie O'Donnell and Deborah Axelrod, M.D., FACS, with Tracy Chutorian Semler (Warner Books, Inc., New York, 1999, $12.99). This book addresses frequently asked questions about breast health and breast cancer in an easy-to-read and lighthearted manner. All of the profits from this book benefit nonprofit organizations, including NABCO. 309 pages. **Bookstores.**

The Breast Book by Dr. Miriam Stoppard (DK Publishing, Inc., New York, 1996, $24.95). This comprehensive, well-illustrated guide to breast care provides women with useful information about all stages of the disease, with particular emphasis on early detection and treatment of breast cancer. 208 pages. **Bookstores.**

Breast Cancer: The Complete Guide by Yashar Hirshaut, M.D., and Peter Pressman, M.D. (Bantam, New York, 1996 edition, paperback $14.95; updated edition expected in September 2000). An easy-to-follow resource providing up-to-date medical information and practical advice on breast cancer, from suspicion of disease through diagnosis, treatment and follow-up care. Dr. Pressman is a member of NABCO's Medical Advisory Board and the foreword is by Amy Langer, Executive Director of NABCO. 334 pages. **Bookstores.**

A Cancer Survivor's Almanac edited by Barbara Hoffman, J.D. (John Wiley and Sons, New York, Second Edition, 1998, $17.00 plus $5.00 shipping). This reference volume from the National Coalition for Cancer Survivorship includes thorough and understandable information about public and private health insurance, survivorship issues, disability benefits, employment rights and legal and financial

Lisa's Story

concerns. 365 pages. **Bookstores,** or contact the **NCCS** at **(888) 937-6227** or www.cansearch.org.

Diagnosis Cancer: Your Guide Through the First Few Months by Wendy Schlessel Harpham, M.D. (W. W. Norton & Co., New York, 1997, paperback $13.00). A valuable guide for newly diagnosed cancer patients, written by an internist who is also a cancer survivor. Includes explanations of and techniques for the different diagnostic tests, administration of chemotherapy drugs and abbreviations used commonly by doctors. 136 pages. **Bookstores.**

Dr. Susan Love's Breast Book by Susan M. Love, M.D., with Karen Lindsey (Addison Wesley, Reading, MA, 1995 revised edition, paperback $17.00). A breast surgeon discusses all conditions of the breast, from benign to malignant. The author's viewpoint on treatment options and controversies is clearly presented in a friendly, accessible style. A good general reference. 657 pages. **Bookstores.**

I Can Cope: Staying Healthy with Cancer by Judi Johnson and Linda Klein (Chronimed Publishing, Minneapolis, MN, 1994, paperback $9.95). The founders of ACS's eight-week "I Can Cope" program have revised and updated their guide to self-help during cancer treatment, using the experiences of several cancer patients. 352 pages. **Bookstores.**

Brochures and Fact Sheets

"Early Detection Brochure" is published annually by the Board of Sponsors of October's National Breast Cancer Awareness Month. This free English/Spanish leaflet discusses breast cancer facts, detection and screening guidelines. Contact **National Breast Cancer Awareness Month, 1800 Concord Pike, Wilmington, DE 19850-5437** or **www.nbcam.org.**

"Facts about Breast Cancer in the USA" (NABCO, February 2000). This free one-page NABCO fact sheet offers the latest basic statistics. Contact **NABCO, (888) 80-NABCO** or **www.nabco.org.**

"Myth or Fact?" (NABCO, August 1999). This free brochure corrects ten common myths about breast cancer. Call **NABCO, (888) 80-NABCO.**

NABCO'S "Things to Know about Breast Cancer" series (1999). A series of free fact sheets about breast cancer risk, early detection, treatment and follow-up care. Contact **NABCO, (888) 80-NABCO** or **www.nabco.org.**

"Understanding Breast Cancer Treatment" (P458, July 1998). This free National Cancer Institute booklet contains lists of questions that will help a patient talk to her doctor about breast cancer. Breast cancer topics covered include: early detection, diagnosis, treatment, adjuvant therapy and reconstruction. Seventy-two pages. Call the **NCI's CIS, (800) 4-CANCER.**

"What You Need to Know about Breast Cancer" (P017, August 1998). The NCI's free comprehensive booklet on breast cancer covering symptoms, diagnosis, treatment, emotional issues and questions to ask your doctor. Includes a glossary. Forty-four pages. Call the **NCI's CIS, (800) 4-CANCER.**

"What You Need to Know about Cancer" (P018, August 1998). The NCI's free overview booklet about cancer—what it is, who is at risk and common treatments. Thirty-three pages. Call the **NCI's CIS, (800) 4-CANCER.**

Lisa's Story

For a listing of support groups contact **NABCO, (888)-80-NABCO** or **www.nabco.org.**

National Alliance of Breast Cancer Organizations (NABCO) is the leading nonprofit resource for information and education about breast cancer, and acts as an advocate for breast cancer patients' and survivors' needs and concerns. Organizations and Friends of NABCO who join NABCO's network receive the quarterly *NABCO News,* customized information packets, other publications, this resource list and special mailings. Membership is tax-deductible to the extent permitted by law; NABCO is rated "9 out of 9" by the National Charities Information Bureau. For more information about membership contact **NABCO, 9 East 37th Street, 10th Floor, New York, NY 10016, (888) 80-NABCO** or **www.nabco.org.**

AMC Cancer Research Center's Cancer Information and Counseling Line has professional cancer counselors who offer easy-to-understand answers to questions about cancer and will mail free instructive publications upon request. Equipped for deaf and hearing-impaired callers. Call the Counseling Line Monday through Friday, 8:30 am to 5:00 pm, **(800) 525-3777.**

American Cancer Society's nationwide toll-free hot line provides information on all forms of cancer, and referrals for the ACS-sponsored "Reach to Recovery" program. Call the **ACS, (800) ACS-2345.**

Cancer Care, Inc. is staffed by social work professionals offering support services, education, information, referrals and financial assistance. Cancer Care's toll-free counseling line assists cancer patients nationwide, and telephone support groups and seminars are available on many topics. Contact **Cancer Care, (800) 813-HOPE, (212) 719-0263 (fax),** or **www.cancercare.org.**

The Cancer Information Service (CIS) of the National Cancer Institute is a national information and education network that provides information and direction on all aspects of cancer. Provides the informational brochures indicated on this list without charge, and refers callers to medical centers and clinical trial programs. Spanish-speaking staff members are available. Call the NCI's CIS at **(800) 4-CANCER.**

Judges and Lawyers Breast Cancer Alert is a confidential hot line for judges, lawyers and law students who have been diagnosed with breast cancer. Contact **JALBCA, 50 King Street, Suite 6D, New York, NY 10014.**

The National Self-Help Clearinghouse will refer callers to regional self-help services. Send a stamped, self-addressed envelope to **National Self-Help Clearinghouse, Graduate School and University Center of the City of New York, 365 5th Avenue, Suite 3300, New York, NY 10016, (212) 817-1822, info@selfhelpweb.org** or **www.selfhelpweb.org.**

Pregnant with Cancer offers hope and support to women who are facing a diagnosis of cancer while pregnant. Contact **Pregnant with Cancer, P.O. Box 1243, Buffalo, NY 14220, (800) 743-6724** or **www.pregnantwithcancer.org.**

The Wellness Community has extensive support and education programs which encourage emotional recovery and wellness. Several locations across the country. All services are free. To find a program near you, contact the national office at **35 East 7th Street, Cincinnati, OH 45202, (888) 793-WELL,** or **www.cancer-support.org.**

Lisa's Story

Y-ME National Breast Cancer Organization offers breast cancer information, support and facility referrals through their national toll-free hot line, **(800) 221-2141 (24 hours; Spanish language line, (800) 986-9505).** Trained peer counselors, all of whom have had breast cancer, are matched by background and experience to callers whenever possible. Y-ME offers information on establishing local support programs, and has twenty-three chapters nationwide, in addition to the national headquarters in Chicago. Y-ME also has a hot line for men whose partners have had breast cancer. Contact **Y-ME, 212 W. Van Buren Street, Chicago, IL 60607** or **www.y-me.org.**

The YWCA of the USA's ENCOREplus Program, located in member associations throughout the country, provides early detection, outreach, education, post-diagnostic support and exercise services to all women. For the location of the program nearest you, contact **ENCOREplus, (800) 95-EPLUS** or **www. ywca.org.**

NAVIGATING YOUR INSURANCE PLAN

Dealing with your health insurance or managed care company can be a trying experience under the best of circumstances, and can be overwhelming while coping with breast cancer at the same time. You will have the best results if you know where to go to get your questions answered or problems resolved. The following advice should help with the most common insurance questions or concerns:

- Check your Benefits Handbook.

- Direct your questions to the Customer or Patient Service office of your insurance or managed care company. Keep a log of your contacts, with date, time, subject, and names.

- If your concerns are still not satisfactorily addressed, you may need to contact the government agency that regulates your insurance plan. If you are covered by a commercial insurance company, your plan is regulated by your State Department of Insurance, listed in the blue pages of your telephone book. However, if your group policy is an *employee benefit* or *self-insured plan* (as are most group plans covering more than a few hundred people), it is regulated by the **U.S. Department of Labor, Pension & Welfare Benefits Administration** at **(202) 254-7013. The Patient Advocate Foundation, 753 Thimble Shoals Boulevard, Suite B, Newport News, VA 23606,** is another good resource for answers to health insurance and managed care questions; call **(800) 532-5274** or **www.patientadvocate.org.**

- Medicare beneficiaries should obtain a copy of *Your Medicare Handbook* from the HCFA, federal agency that administers Medicare. Write to the **Health Care Finance Administration, 6325 Security Boulevard, Baltimore, MD 21207,** or call the **National Medicare Hotline** at **(800) MEDICARE,** or the **Social Security Administration** at **(800) 772-3736.**

Insurance Resources

"**Cancer Treatments Your Insurance Should Cover**" (April 1995). This free brochure describes standard and investigational treatments that should be covered, and what to do if reimbursement is denied. Eight pages. Available at **www.accc-cancer.org.**

Lisa's Story

The Consumer's Guides (1999). Comprehensive, free guides to understanding insurance for disability, health and long-term care. Contact the **Health Insurance Association of America (HIAA), (888) 869-4078, (202) 824-1849** or **www. hiaa.org.**

"The Managed Care Answer Guide" (1997, $4.50 each). A consumer publication of the Patient Advocate Foundation is a reference handbook that includes a glossary of terms, coverage information and other facts for cancer patients insured by managed care plans. Thirty-five pages. Also available in Spanish. Contact the **Patient Advocate Foundation, 753 Thimble Shoals Boulevard, Suite B, Newport News, VA 23606, (800) 532-5274, (757) 873-6668** or **www.patientadvocate.org.**

The National Insurance Consumer Helpline is a hot line that answers consumer questions, and offers problem-solving support and printed materials including information on life and property casualty insurance. Call **(800) 942-4242.** Open 8:00 am to 8:00 pm Eastern Standard Time, Monday through Friday.

"What Cancer Survivors Need to Know about Health Insurance" (1999). Provides a clear understanding of health insurance and how to receive maximum reimbursement for claims. Twenty-nine pages. Contact the **National Coalition for Cancer Survivorship, (888) 650-9127,** or www@cansearch.org. The NCCS also publishes *A Cancer Survivor's Almanac*, which contains useful information about insurance coverage.

OBTAINING FINANCIAL ASSISTANCE

Financial assistance with breast cancer treatment for patients who are **uninsured** or **underinsured** can be difficult to obtain. Here are some possible resources to get you started:

- **Start at the hospital where you are receiving your care.** Speak with a financial counselor at the hospital and describe your situation. Often, a payment schedule can be arranged. Inform the counselor of the steps you are taking to gain assistance, and remain in contact with this counselor as the process moves forward. Keep a record of each conversation, the date and topics discussed.

- Speak with your **hospital social worker.** This person will help you initiate the process of obtaining insurance coverage, Medicaid, public assistance, food stamps, Social Security and other benefits for which you may be eligible. This professional should also be knowledgeable about local community organizations that provide financial assistance. Be assertive and bring questions prepared in advance.

- **Public assistance,** such as **Medicaid,** may be available if you are ineligible for other programs. Call your local **Social Services Department** or the **Department of Public Welfare** for information on public assistance programs.

- You may be eligible for **Supplemental Security Income (SSI)** and/or **Social Security** benefits. While receiving SSI, you could also be eligible for food stamps and Medicaid. For information, and to set up a time to speak with a representative who can help you get started, ask your hospital social worker or call the **Social Security Administration at (800) 772-1213.**

Lisa's Story

- Some states sell health insurance to people with serious medical conditions who cannot find insurance elsewhere. Contact your **State Department of Insurance** or **State Department of Health** to see if your state has a program for the "hard to insure."

- The **Hill-Burton Program** may provide you with some assistance. This is a federal program that requires participating hospitals to provide a predetermined amount of free care or reduced-fee care to people unable to pay. This program is not available at all hospitals, and each hospital determines what type of care is made available. Call your hospital or **(800) 638-0742** for information, or **www.hrsa.dhhs.gov/osp/dfcr/**.

- The **American Cancer Society** office in your area can provide information on local sources of financial assistance. Check your telephone directory for the number.

- Some **pharmaceutical companies** have **assistance programs** that provide necessary drugs to people who cannot afford them. Most of these programs must usually be accessed through the prescribing physician. However, you may be able to expedite the process and, in some cases, apply directly by having information sent to you. Contact the **Pharmaceutical Research and Manufacturers of America, 1100 15th Street, NW, Washington, DC 20005, (800) PMA-INFO** or **www.pharma.org**. If the company that makes the drug you need is not in this directory, your physician or social worker may know of other assistance programs.

- **Cancer Care, Inc.,** has a toll-free counseling line staffed with trained social workers who can suggest referrals for financial assistance. The **"AVONCares"**

program at Cancer Care provides financial assistance for diagnostic and support services. Contact **Cancer Care, (800) 813-HOPE** or **www.cancercare.org.**

Financial and Legal Matters

AIRLIFELINE contact **(877) AIR-LIFE** or **www.airlifeline.org;** **Corporate Angel Network** contact **Westchester County Airport, 1 Loop Road, White Plains, NY 10604, (914) 328-1313** or **www.corpangelnetwork.org** and **The National Patient Travel Center** contact **(800) 296-1217** or **www.patienttravel.org** are services that provide or connect qualifying individuals who are undergoing treatment for cancer with free air travel. Each organization has slightly different services and requirements for qualification.

American Preferred Prescription at **(800) 227-1195; Bio Logics—The Rx Resource** at **(800) 850-4306; Managed Rx Plans, Inc.,** at **(800) 799-8765** and **AMD Pharmacy** at **(800) 873-9773** are services that ship medications by mail. Each service has different policies regarding insurance, payment and shipping. Call each directly for more information.

The Breast Health Access for Women with Disabilities Project is providing direct services and public and professional education for this population. The Project is headquartered at **Alta Bates Medical Center, Department of Rehabilitation, 2001 Dwight Way, 2nd Floor, Berkeley, CA 94704, (510) 204-4866** or **www.bhawd.org.**

Five Wishes is an online living will from Aging with Dignity that is legal in thirty-three states and Washington, DC. Web site includes advice on establish-

Lisa's Story

ing surrogate, advance directives and related topics. Available at **www.agingwithdignity.org.**

The Job Accommodation Network provides information on employees' rights under the Americans with Disabilities Act. Contact the **Network, (800) ADA-WORK** or **www.jan.wvu.edu.**

Surviving the Legal Challenges: A Resource Guide for Women with Breast Cancer (California Women's Law Center, 1998, Free to breast cancer survivors, otherwise $10.00). General reference (with some issues specific to the state of California) on women's legal rights. Eighty-five pages. Contact the **Center, (213) 637-9900** or **www.cwlc.org.**

HOW TO FIND A BREAST CANCER SUPPORT GROUP

If you cannot locate a convenient support group from NABCO's comprehensive listing of groups at **www.nabco.org:**

- Inquire at a **local major hospital's Breast Center** or departments of Social Work or Psychiatry.

- Call the National Cancer Institute's Cancer Information Service at **(800) 4-CANCER** for the names of FDA-certified mammography providers in your area, and ask these providers for support group suggestions.

- Contact your local **American Cancer Society** office or **(800) ACS-2345** for local groups that ACS or others sponsor.

- Call a group on NABCO's list in your state and ask if they know of any groups located nearer to you.

Please note: Some people benefit more from individual counseling than from group support.

3. Facing Breast Cancer—Surgical and Radiation Treatment Options

You have breast cancer. But the good news is that you have a number of choices for treatment, and you and your doctor are partners. Remember, after the biopsy, much of the breast cancer has been removed, so DON'T RUSH into treatment, although NABCO recommends that you have a clear action plan in place within a few weeks after initial diagnosis. Here are the most important things you'll want to think about:

- *Confidence in the expertise of your medical team.* Be sure that your physician is a breast cancer expert—although many surgeons operate on breasts, you will receive the best care from a truly experienced surgeon who is a breast specialist, or from a surgical oncologist, who is fully up to date in this rapidly changing field. Take the time to get a second opinion, to hire and fire, if you are not fully confident in the skills of the surgical team that often begins a woman's definitive medical treatment for breast cancer.

- *Comfort with your medical team.* Be certain that you are comfortable with and can communicate well with your team. You need to understand exactly what to

Lisa's Story

expect with each treatment, and what both the short- and long-term effects of therapy will be, on your body and on your life. If you do not feel that your questions are being answered completely and satisfactorily, consider finding a new surgeon.

- *Choose the treatment that's right for you.* If you are able to choose it and are comfortable with it, breast-conserving treatment is the option that most women report as the least physically disruptive. However, you should "try on" a number of options, and talk them over with the people who know you best.

HOW TO FIND A BREAST SPECIALIST

NABCO recommends selecting a board-certified surgical breast specialist or surgical oncologist to perform definitive surgery once breast cancer has been confirmed by biopsy. To find a breast specialist:

- Ask your family doctor or gynecologist for a referral. Your doctor can also contact the **American Society of Clinical Oncology** at **(703) 299-0150** or **www.asco.org** or the **Society of Surgical Oncology** at **(847) 427-1400** to be referred to local surgical oncologists who are ASCO or SSO members. **The American Board of Medical Specialties** at **(800) 776-2378** or **www.certifieddoctor.org** can verify a physician's board certification by specialty and year, and will refer callers to local board-certified doctors. Many State Health Departments now maintain a "Consumer Information" section of their web sites that includes an updated, alphabetical listing of state physicians who have been cited for professional misconduct.

*Resources*

- Call the **National Cancer Institute's Cancer Information Service, (800) 4-CANCER** for the names of NCI-affiliated treatment centers in your state, including members of the NCI's CCOP program. If none of these centers is conveniently located, call the Department of Surgery at the nearest one and ask for a local referral.

- **Ask-a-Nurse** is a free service providing twenty-four-hour health care information and referrals from registered nurses in select locations around the country. Call **(800) 535-1111** to find out if there is an office in your area, and ask if they will refer over the telephone.

- For referrals to a plastic surgeon for corrective or reconstructive procedures, contact the **American Society of Plastic Surgeons'** referral service at **(800) 635-0635** or **www.plasticsurgery.org** for a list of local board-certified plastic surgeons.

Lymphedema

The National Lymphedema Network is a nonprofit organization providing information about the prevention and treatment of lymphedema to patients and health care professionals, as well as support groups. Contact the Network, **1611 Telegraph Avenue, Suite 1111 Oakland, CA 94612, (800) 541-3259, (510) 208-3110** (fax), or **www.lymphnet.org**.

Lymphedema: A Breast Cancer Patient's Guide to Prevention and Healing by Jeannie Burt and Gwen White, P.T. (Hunter House Publishers, Berkeley, CA, 1999, $12.95) describes the options women have for treating lymphedema. 204 pages. **Bookstores,** or call **(800) 266-5592**.

Lisa's Story

- **Prostheses (Breast forms).** Although this list includes a few mail-order services experienced in working over the telephone, having a trained fitter discuss and respond to your needs is often the best approach. The lingerie areas in some department stores employ professional fitters who will help you find a comfortable and suitable prosthesis, and a bra to wear with it. Smaller lingerie boutiques in major cities often perform this function—check your local Yellow Pages under "Lingerie" or "Brassieres," or in larger cities, under "Breast Prostheses." Prostheses may also be ordered from selected surgical supply stores, often listed under "Surgical Appliances and Supplies." Temporary prostheses can be ordered by mail. Women who cannot afford a prosthesis may contact the Y-ME Prosthesis Bank or the Breast Cancer Resource Center of the Princeton YWCA. (See below.)

- **Bathing suits and lingerie.** Contact the sources mentioned above. In addition, a number of specialty boutiques sell clothing with post-mastectomy needs in mind, although there is not yet a national chain. Consult the Yellow Pages under "Lingerie." If you have difficulty locating a local retailer, contact the Reach-to-Recovery volunteer at your nearest American Cancer Society office, ask at a local breast cancer support group, or contact the social work department at your largest local hospital.

Personal Resources: External Prostheses

Breast Cancer Resource Center of the Princeton YWCA offers free wigs and breast forms to women in financial need nationwide. Shipping must be prepaid.

Contact the **Breast Cancer Resource Center**, 914 Commons Way, Princeton, NJ 08540, (609) 252-2003 or www.princetonol.com/groups/ywca.

Lady Grace Stores is a chain of post–breast surgery stores with locations in Massachusetts, New Hampshire and Maine. Mail orders available for a full line of lingerie, bras, girdles, swimwear, leisure wear and breast forms. Medicare accepted in some cases. Publishes a newsletter. Contact **Lady Grace, (800) 922-0504** or **www.ladygrace.com**.

Lands' End Catalog national retailer offers five different styles of specially designed mastectomy swimwear. Call **(800) 356-4444.**

Women's Health Boutiques are a retail chain staffed with certified fitters and women's health specialists that offers one-stop shopping for women following breast surgery. Breast forms, lingerie, wigs and other products and services are available. Medicare, Medicaid and private insurance are accepted. For the location nearest you, call **(800) 494-2374.**

Y-ME Prosthesis and Wig Bank is available for women in financial need. If the appropriate size is available, Y-ME will mail a wig and/or breast prosthesis anywhere in the country. The organization's twenty-four-hour hot line is staffed with breast cancer survivors. A nominal handling fee is requested. Call **Y-ME, (800) 221-2141.**

Breast Reconstruction

A Woman's Decision: Breast Care, Treatment and Reconstruction by Karen Berger and John Bostwick III, M.D., (Quality Medical Publishing, Inc., St. Louis, MO, Third Edition, 1998, $18.50). A comprehensive resource about breast can-

Lisa's Story

cer surgical options and reconstructive surgery. Also includes interviews with survivors who discuss their results. 575 pages. **Bookstores,** or call **Quality Medical Publishing, (800) 348-7808.** Also available, **"What Women Want to Know about Breast Implants"** ($6.00). Highlights from *A Woman's Decision: Breast Care, Treatment and Reconstruction.* Fifty-seven pages. Call **Quality Medical Publishing, (800) 348-7808.**

"Breast Implants: An Information Update 1998" (The U.S. Food and Drug Administration). Contact the **FDA, (800) INFO-FDA** or **www.fda.gov/cdrh/breastimplants/.**

Breast Implants: Everything You Need to Know by Nancy Bruning (Hunter House, Alameda, CA, 1995, paperback $12.95). A valuable resource for any woman considering breast implants, or for those who have them. Includes details of potential health risks, alternatives to implants and advice on when and whether to remove them. A resource list is included. 202 pages. **Bookstores,** or contact **Hunter House, (800) 266-5592,** or **ordering@hunterhouse.com.**

"Breast Reconstruction after Mastectomy" (4630, 1998). Describes types of surgery with photographs and drawings, and gives answers to commonly asked questions as well as a glossary of terms. Eighteen pages. Call the **ACS, (800) ACS-2345.**

"Information for Women about the Safety of Silicone Implants" (Institute of Medicine, 2000). Highlights from the IOM committee's definitive report that concluded that silicone breast implants did not cause disease or cancer. Thirty pages. Call **Y-ME, (800) 221-2141.**

Resources

"Options in Breast Reconstruction" (Mentor H/S, Inc., 5425 Hollister Avenue, Santa Barbara, CA 93111). This free video and companion brochure review the options of using one's own tissue, implants, or no reconstruction at all. Thirty-five minutes. Contact **Mentor H/S, (800) MENTOR-8,** or **www.mentorcorp.com.**

Radiation Therapy

"**NIH Consensus Conference Statement: Treatment of Early Stage Breast Cancer**" (June 1990, volume 8, number 6). Still the current standard, the surgical and other treatment recommendations of the expert panel convened by the National Institutes of Health. The roles of mastectomy versus breast conservation, adjuvant systemic therapy and the use of prognostic indicators in the treatment and management of early-stage breast cancer are evaluated. Available at **odp.od.nih.gov/consensus** (no "www" is needed).

"**Radiation Therapy and You: A Guide to Self-Help During Treatment**" (P123, 1997). This booklet clearly explains the external and internal forms of radiation therapy. Fifty-two pages. Call the **NCI's CIS, (800) 4-CANCER.**

THE COMPUTER-FRIENDLY BREAST CANCER SURVIVOR

Online information seekers should visit NABCO's web site at **www.nabco.org.** NABCO's site has news, special features, programs, extensive resources and references. These include Fact Sheets, *NABCO News* editions, excerpts from our *Resource List,* includ-

Lisa's Story

ing the directory of local support groups, and links to numerous other web sites of interest.

Since breast cancer information on the web changes rapidly, we recommend that in addition to NABCO, you begin at the following reputable sites that maintain good current links to other web sites:

- Can Search (National Coalition for Cancer Survivorship): **www.cansearch.org**

- National Action Plan on Breast Cancer: **www.napbc.org**

- The National Cancer Institute: **cancernet.nci.nih.gov** (no "www" needed)

- NCI's Cancer Trials: **cancertrials.nci.nih.gov** (no "www" needed)

- Oncolink: **cancer.med.upenn.edu** (no "www" needed)

- US Department of Health and Human Services–National Women's Health Information Center: **www.4woman.org**

Also visit **www.hersource.com,** the new web site for women and breast cancer professionals being developed by General Electric Medical Systems.

- **Computer Bulletin Boards and Listserves.** Commercial online services have brought the cancer community to a new level of wide availability of cancer support and information. *America Online* **(800) 827-6364,** and *CompuServe* **(800) 848-8199,** have bulletin boards where cancer survivors exchange support and information. E-mail users can subscribe to breast cancer electronic support groups and mailing lists where breast cancer patients, family and friends, and health professionals share information and advice through e-mail messages.

- **Searches.** You can search online broadly through the main search engines, if you are willing to sort through the large volume of information you will receive in return. Major search engines include **www.altavista.com, www.infoseek.com, www.msn.com** and **www.yahoo.com. Excite** at **www.excite.com** offers the capability of searching by concept rather than by keyword.

- You can also perform online **literature searches.** *Medline* is the largest online database, with 3,600 contributing medical journals, and has a separate database called *Cancerlit.* Many public libraries and medical libraries subscribe and will permit searches, sometimes for a fee. *Medline* is available at no cost on the web through **HealthGate** at **www.healthgate.com.** You can also use special software such as *Grateful Med* at **igm.nlm.nih.gov** (no "www" is needed).

4. Facing Breast Cancer—Systemic and Medical Treatment Options

In addition to using surgery and radiation to treat the breast, underarm lymph nodes and chest area, known as "local" therapy, your doctor may also suggest that you consider options for treating any breast cancer cells that could be elsewhere in your body. "Systemic" treatment uses chemotherapy and hormonal therapy either in a preventative way, just in case any cancer cells have left the chest area, known as "adjuvant" therapy, or to treat cancer found

Lisa's Story

outside the chest area when breast cancer is first diagnosed. Here are the most important things you'll want to know about:

- *Lifestyle during treatment.* Side effects vary, and drugs that manage the side effects of chemotherapy have advanced to the point that many women continue their work and home lives during treatment. Although it's important to ask what to expect, treatment will vary for each woman.

- *Practical planning during treatment.* Some treatment reactions, however, are certain, and can be prepared for. These may include ordering a wig in anticipation of hair loss; arranging for more help at home or on the job for when treatment makes you tired; assistance with insurance and reimbursement matters; and planning for support and resources to help you cope with the emotional side effects of breast cancer treatment and diagnosis. The emotional aspects are every bit as urgent, important and real as the physical side effects.

- *Clinical trials.* Without question, progress would be made more quickly in breast cancer research if a greater number of breast cancer patients received treatment on clinical trials. If your physician suggests that you consider being part of a research study, explore this alternative carefully. Well-designed studies compare current state-of-the-art treatment with researchers' best hope for improvement in the future.

Chemotherapy and Hormonal Therapy

Bone Marrow Transplants: A Book of Basics for Patients by Susan K. Stewart (BMT Newsletter, Highland Park, IL, 1995, $7.95 plus shipping). Written by a former

BMT patient and editor of the *Blood & Marrow Transplant Newsletter,* this book compiles articles from back issues of the newsletter to provide essential information for patients considering BMT, stem cell or cord blood transplantation and for those who have undergone the procedure. Includes a chapter on insurance issues and an excellent resource list. 157 pages. Contact the **Blood & Marrow Transplant Newsletter, 2900 Skokie Valley Road, Suite B, Highland Park, IL 60035, (888) 579-7674 or (847) 433-4599** (fax)**, help@bmtnews.org,** or **www.bmtnews.org.**

"Chemotherapy and You: A Guide to Self-Help During Treatment" (P117, 1997). This booklet, in question-and-answer format, addresses concerns of patients receiving chemotherapy. Emphasis is on explanation, self-help and participation during treatment. Includes a glossary. Fifty-six pages. Call the **NCI's CIS, (800) 4-CANCER.**

A Guide to Good Nutrition During and After Chemotherapy and Radiation by Saundra N. Aker, R.D., and Polly Lennsen, R.D., M.S. (Third Edition, 1988, $8.00 plus $3.00 shipping). A practical approach to patient nutrition, with helpful hints and specific dietary suggestions for controlling appetite and digestion-related problems. 147 pages. Quantity discounts available. Contact the **Fred Hutchinson Cancer Research Center Clinical Nutrition Program, 1124 Columbia Street, Room E211, Seattle, WA 98104, (206) 667-4834.**

"Helping Yourself During Chemotherapy: 4 Steps for Patients" (P603, 1994). This easy-to-read brochure suggests four steps to follow during chemotherapy treatment. Twelve pages. Call the **NCI's CIS, (800) 4-CANCER.**

Managing the Side Effects of Chemotherapy and Radiation Therapy: A Guide for Patients and Their Families by Marylin J. Dodd, R.N., Ph.D. (UCSF

Lisa's Story

Nursing Press, San Francisco, Third Edition, 1996, $20.00 plus $6.00 shipping). This easy-to-read book details the possible side effects and symptoms of chemotherapy and radiation therapy, offering specific suggestions for managing each side effect. 190 pages. Contact **UCSF Nursing Press, 521 Parnassus Avenue, Room N535C, San Francisco, CA 94143-0608, (415) 476-4991,** or **(415) 476-6042** (fax).

"Progress for Life" (AstraZeneca Pharmaceuticals, 1996). A free educational package that includes written materials and a video that answers frequently asked questions about treatment with tamoxifen. Also includes general information on breast cancer and toll-free numbers for information resources. Contact **AstraZeneca, (800) 34-LIFE-4,** or **www.astrazeneca.com.**

"Questions and Answers about Tamoxifen" (1999). A fact sheet on tamoxifen and its side effects. Four pages. Call the **NCI's CIS, (800) 4-CANCER.**

"Understanding Chemotherapy" (1998, 9456). This booklet provides a brief introduction to chemotherapy, its benefits and side effects. Call the **ACS, (800) ACS-2345.**

Managing Side Effects of Chemotherapy Treatment

Beauty of Control with Jill Eikenberry and created by Laurie Feldman (1995, $19.95 plus $5.45 shipping). A video about the cosmetic and emotional side effects of cancer treatments. Seventeen minutes. Contact **Medical Video Productions, 450 North New Ballas Road, Suite 266, St. Louis, MO 63141, (800) 822-3100.**

Resources

Becoming, Inc. is a catalog filled with lingerie, workout wear, swimsuits, wigs, breast forms and accessories. Two percent of profits go to breast cancer awareness and research programs. For a catalog of products, call **(800) 980-9085.**

Edith Imre Foundation for Loss of Hair provides counseling and support as well as a selection of appropriate wigs. Patients can request financial assistance through their physicians. Contact the **Foundation, 30 West 57th Street, 2nd Floor, New York, NY 10019.** For appointments, call **(212) 757-8160** or for information, call the **Wig Hotline, (212) 765-8397.**

Look Good . . . Feel Better is a public service program sponsored by the Cosmetic, Toiletry and Fragrance Association Foundation in partnership with ACS and the National Cosmetology Association. It helps women manage changes in their appearance resulting from cancer treatment. The program's print and videotape materials are available both to patients and to health professionals. Instructional sessions run by ACS are offered in a number of locations. Materials are also available in Spanish. Call **(800) 395-LOOK** or **(800) ACS-2345.**

Making Treatment Choices

AstraZeneca Pharmaceuticals Patient Education Service offers free patient education materials on risk reduction, breast cancer and tamoxifen therapy. Contact **AstraZeneca Pharmaceuticals, 1800 Concord Pike, Wilmington, DE 19850 (800) 34-LIFE-4,** or **www.astrazeneca.com.**

Cancerfax® is a way to access NCI's Physician's Data Query (PDQ) system (see entry below) via fax machine, twenty-four hours a day, seven days a week, at no

Lisa's Story

charge other than the charge for the fax call. Two versions of the treatment information are available: one for health care professionals and the other for patients, family or the general public. Information also available in Spanish. To obtain instructions and list of necessary codes, call **(301) 402-5874.** If there are problems with the fax, call **(800) 624-7890.** Obtain code information by phone through the **NCI's CIS, (800) 4-CANCER,** or **cancernet.nci.nih.gov** (no "www" is needed).

Cancertrials is a new, up-to-date NCI resource on the web that is all about clinical trials for cancer. It is easy to use and navigate, and was designed to help users find and choose a treatment trial, and offers news about research discoveries. Available at **cancertrials.nci.nih.gov** (no "www" is needed).

Community Clinical Oncology Program (CCOP) is a network of the forty-eight medical centers in thirty-six states and Puerto Rico that have been selected by the National Cancer Institute to introduce new clinical protocols and to accrue patients to clinical trials at the community level. Especially useful for patients who do not live near an NCI-affiliated cancer center. Call the **NCI's CIS at (800) 4-CANCER** to receive contact information for **CCOP** institutions in your area.

National Cancer Institute (NCI) Designated Cancer Centers are institutions that have been recognized by the NCI for their work in creating new and innovative approaches to cancer research. For a listing of Cancer Centers in your community, contact the **NCI's CIS at (800) 4-CANCER,** or **www.nci.nih.gov/cancercenters/.**

"Patient to Patient: Cancer Clinical Trials and You" (V112). This video provides simple information for patients and families about clinical trials. Fifteen minutes. Produced in collaboration with the American College of Surgeons Commission on Cancer. Call the **NCI's CIS, (800) 4-CANCER.**

Resources

Physician Data Query (PDQ) is the computerized cancer database of the NCI, that provides information on treatment, organizations, doctors involved in cancer care and a listing of more than 1,500 clinical trials that are open to patient accrual. For more information, contact the **NCI's CIS** at **(800) 4-CANCER**, or **cancernet. nci.nih.gov** (no "www" is needed).

"Taking Part in Clinical Trials: What Cancer Patients Need to Know" (P148, 1998). A booklet designed for patients who are considering participating in cancer trials, with explanations in easy-to-understand terms and information that will help them to reach an appropriate decision. Includes a glossary. Eighteen pages. Also available in Spanish (P029). Call the **NCI's CIS, (800) 4-CANCER.**

JOINING A CLINICAL TRIAL

Today, fewer than 5 percent of breast cancer patients receive treatment for their disease as part of a clinical trial. Clinical trials offer the best method to monitor and measure benefits of treatment and its side effects, ultimately improving breast cancer treatment for all patients in the future.

What a clinical trial is, trial advantages and trade-offs and how to enroll in a trial are often not well understood by women with breast cancer.

- The NCI's PDQ database offers **extensive information** on treatment trials. Information is available at **(800) 4-CANCER, (301) 402-5874** (fax), or **cancertrials. nci.nih.gov** (no "www" is needed). You may request English or Spanish, in formats designed for patients and for professionals.

Lisa's Story

Alternative Therapies

NABCO does not endorse any therapy for breast cancer that has not been subjected to rigorous levels of clinical verification and peer review. Prior to any involvement with alternative treatment programs, NABCO recommends that you thoroughly investigate the treatment's background, and that you discuss your intentions and questions with your physician.

The Alternative Medicine Homepage is a web site that links to information sources about alternative and complementary therapies at **www.pitt.edu/~cbw/altm.html.**

Center for Mind-Body Medicine has become a leader in promoting "complementary" cancer care, the term for treatments that combine standard treatments with alternative approaches. Contact the **Center, 5225 Connecticut Avenue NW, Suite 414, Washington, DC 20015, (202) 966-7338, (202) 966-2589** (fax), or **www.cmbm.org.**

Choices in Healing: Integrating the Best of Conventional and Complementary Approaches to Cancer by Michael Lerner (MIT Press, Cambridge, MA, 1994, hardcover $45.00, 1996, paperback $20.00). Greeted with enthusiasm by health professionals in both the mainstream and alternative health communities, this book is useful for those interested in considering alternative therapies in conjunction with standard medical treatment. 626 pages. **Bookstores.**

National Center for Complementary and Alternative Medicine at the National Institutes of Health investigates alternative medical treatments, helps integrate effective treatment into mainstream medical practice and offers information packages. Contact **NCCAM Clearinghouse, PO Box 8218, Silver Spring, MD**

20907-8218, (888) 644-6226, (301) 495-4957 (fax), or **nccam.nih.gov** (no "www" is needed).

The National Cancer Institute Complementary and Alternative Medicine web site provides information summaries on complementary and alternative therapies at **cancernet.nci.nih.gov/treatment/cam.shtml** (no "www" is needed).

The National Foundation for Alternative Medicine investigates, collects and publicizes information on effective alternative medical treatments. Contact **The National Foundation for Alternative Medicine, 1629 K Street NW, Suite 402, Washington, DC 20006, (202) 463-4900,** or **www.nfam.org.**

Questionable Nutritional Therapies (233.00, 2000). This paper reviews the treatment of cancer by nutritional means. Call the **ACS, (800) ACS-2345.**

5. Coping with, and Adjusting to, Breast Cancer

Although having breast cancer is a transforming experience, a woman retains her coping style and personality throughout her diagnosis, treatment and recovery. Women adjust to breast cancer using the style and approach they have found most successful for life's major problems. Whatever your personal style may be, following these suggestions will make the process easier, based on the experiences relayed to NABCO by thousands of women:

- *Plan for practical needs.* Few aspects of work, home and family life are unaffected by diagnosis and treatment. Anticipating what changes might occur—using the "worst," or most extreme, case—and planning for them as early as possible frees

Lisa's Story

up the patient to focus on her treatment and her own needs. Consider accepting the offers of help that you will receive so you can delegate practical jobs (such as child or elder care, cooking, or insurance paperwork) to close relatives and friends. This can be a satisfying way to accomplish those jobs while reducing the frustration levels and feelings of helplessness of those around you.

▪ *Seek emotional support.* Since breast cancer often arrives as a symptomless surprise, women are generally unprepared to cope with its practical, medical and emotional impact. NABCO recommends some form of emotional support as a component of each woman's treatment. Additional support for her life partner and family members should be considered, as well. Support can take many forms which often vary with needs over time, and should be chosen based on what fits and feels best: a group setting with other survivors; individual counseling with a therapist or social worker; and spiritual counseling with a religious leader.

▪ *Use the many available resources.* A number of the millions of survivors, women who have "been there," have written about their own ways of coping and adjusting, and many service and nonprofit organizations (including NABCO) help breast cancer survivors have the best quality of life, through treatment and beyond. Resources to help you cope exist on a wide range of subjects, ranging from wig and prosthesis "banks" to tips on protesting a denied health insurance claim. For more extensive listings than those found below, visit NABCO's web site at **www.nabco.org**, or order the complete *NABCO Breast Cancer Resource List* (updated annually) which includes a listing of nearly 700 U.S. regional support groups, organized by state.

You'll want to learn more about . . . emotional recovery, coping, sexuality, family and partner issues and living a healthy lifestyle.

Resources

Breast Cancer in Men is a web site offering information about male breast cancer, online support and chat sessions. Visit **interact.withus.com/interact/mbc** (no "www" is needed).

Cancer Hope Network is a national agency that provides one-to-one emotional support by matching a cancer patient or family with a volunteer who had a similar diagnosis. The volunteer visits over the phone or, where possible, in person, offering emotional support. Services are free and confidential. Contact the **Cancer Hope Network, (877) HOPE-NET, info@cancerhopenetwork.org,** or **www. cancerhopenetwork.org.**

"For Single Women with Breast Cancer" (Y-ME, 1995). A booklet that offers practical guidance and emotional support for women without partners or women who live alone. Single copies available free, bulk orders available on request. Also available in Spanish. Call **Y-ME, (800) 221-2141.**

Not Now . . . I'm Having a No Hair Day: Humor and Healing for People with Cancer by Christine Clifford, illustrated by Jack Lindstrom (Pfeifer-Hamilton, Duluth, MN, 1996, $9.95). Using her own experience with breast cancer, the author shows how the power of laughter and positive thinking can promote recovery and growth. 144 pages. Contact **The Cancer Club, 6533 Limerick Drive, Edina, MN 55439, (800) 586-9062** or **www.cancerclub.com.**

Reach to Recovery is a program of the American Cancer Society. Trained volunteers who themselves have had breast cancer visit newly diagnosed patients. The volunteer provides information and support to the patient during the visit; ser-

Lisa's Story

vices are appropriate after either mastectomy or lumpectomy. To request a visit, call the **ACS, (800) ACS-2345.**

Spinning Straw into Gold: Your Emotional Recovery from Breast Cancer by Ronnie Kaye, MFCC (Simon & Schuster, New York, 1991, paperback $11.00). Written by a psychotherapist who won her own battle with breast cancer, this comprehensive guide to emotional recovery from the disease is based in part on her clients' stories. 181 pages. **Bookstores.**

The Wellness Community Guide to Fighting for Recovery from Cancer by Harold H. Benjamin, Ph.D. (Putnam, New York, 1995, $13.95). This revised and expanded edition describes over thirty practical methods cancer patients can use to hasten recovery. 270 pages. **Bookstores. The Wellness Community** has extensive support and education programs that encourage emotional recovery and a feeling of wellness. Several locations across the country. All services are free. To find a program near you, contact the national office at **35 East 7th Street, Cincinnati, OH 45202, (888) 793-WELL,** or **www.cancer-support.org.**

Coping

A Helping Hand: The Resource Guide for People with Cancer (Cancer Care, Inc., 1997). This handbook provides practical information about the kinds of help available to people with cancer and how to access these resources. Contact **Cancer Care, (800) 813-HOPE, (212) 719-0263** (fax), or **www.cancercare.org.**

The Cancer Club markets humorous and helpful products for people with cancer. These include a quarterly newsletter ($12.95/year), audiocassettes, computer software, mugs, t-shirts, books and videos. Contact **The Cancer Club, 6533 Limerick Drive, Edina, MN 55439, (800) 586-9062, (612) 941-1229** (fax), **canclub@ primenet.com,** or **www.cancerclub.com.**

Caring for the Patient with Cancer at Home: A Guide for Patients and Families (4656, 1996 edition). A guidebook with detailed, helpful information on how to care for the patient at home. Ninety pages. Call the **ACS, (800) ACS-2345.**

Home Care Guide for Cancer (American College of Physicians, $29.95). Written by health care professionals, cancer patients and family members, this book discusses the physical and emotional challenges that a cancer patient may face. Presents home care plans for both the patient and the caregiver. Call the **American College of Physicians, (800) 523-1546, ext. 2600.**

"**Talking with Your Doctor**" (4638-CC, 1997 edition). Suggestions for effective doctor/patient communication. Six pages. Call the **ACS, (800) ACS-2345.**

"**Teamwork: The Cancer Patients' Guide to Talking with Your Doctor**" (National Coalition for Cancer Survivorship, $3.00 for members of the NCCS, $4.00 for non-members). Useful suggestions on how to best begin and maintain a working relationship with a physician that is constructive to both the doctor and the patient. Thirty-two pages. Contact **NCCS, 1010 Wayne Avenue, 5th Floor, Silver Spring, MD 20910, (888) 937-6227,** or **www.cansearch.org.**

Family and Partner Issues: Male Partners

Helping Your Mate Face Breast Cancer by Judy C. Kneece, R.N., OCN (EduCare Publishing, 1995, $12.95 plus $4.50 shipping). A supportive partner's guide to

Lisa's Story

understanding the emotional responses of mates and other family members. Offers helpful suggestions on coping strategies and how to support the physical and emotional recovery of a partner. 133 pages. A companion book is also available, *Your Breast Cancer Treatment Handbook*. Contact **EduCare Publishing, P.O. Box 280305, Columbia, SC 29228, (803) 796-6100**, or **www.cancer-help.com.**

The Well Spouse Foundation is a national, nonprofit membership organization which gives support to husbands, wives and partners of the chronically ill and/or disabled. Support groups and a bimonthly newsletter are available. Contact the **Well Spouse Foundation, 30 East 40th Street, P.H., New York, NY 10016, (800) 838-0879,** or **www.wellspouse.org.**

"When the Woman You Love Has Breast Cancer" (Y-ME, 1994). A booklet that helps partners give emotional support to their loved ones. Single copies available free, bulk orders available on request. Call **Y-ME, (800) 221-2141.**

Y-ME National Breast Cancer Organization has trained male volunteers who provide support and counseling to other male partners of women with breast cancer through their national hot line, **(800) 221-2141** (9:00 am to 5:00 pm CST, Monday through Friday).

Family and Partner Issues: Women Who Partner with Women

Cancer in Two Voices by Sandra Butler and Barbara Rosenblum (Spinsters Book Company, MN, 1996, expanded edition with essay by Sandra Butler, $12.95). This is a particularly moving and honest account of the authors' identity as Jewish

Resources

women and as lesbians as they live with advanced breast cancer, from excerpts in their diaries. 183 pages. **Bookstores.**

The Lesbian Community Cancer Project gives support, information, education, advocacy and direct services to lesbians and women living with cancer and their families. Contact **Lesbian Community Cancer Project, 4753 North Broadway, Suite 602, Chicago, IL 60640-4907, (773) 561-4662,** or **www.iccp.org.**

The Mautner Project for Lesbians with Cancer is a volunteer organization dedicated to helping lesbians with cancer, as well as their partners, and caregivers. The pamphlet **"Lesbians and Cancer"** provides early detection information and addresses issues for lesbians. Available at no cost in English or Spanish from the **Mautner Project, 1707 L Street NW, Suite 500, Washington, DC 20036, (202) 332-5536, mautner@mautnerproject.org** or **www. mautnerproject.org.**

Family and Partner Issues: Family and Friends

"Handbook for Mothers Supporting Daughters with Breast Cancer" (1999). Handbook that offers practical advice and sources of information to the mothers of women with breast cancer. Twenty-six pages. Contact **Mothers Supporting Daughters with Breast Cancer, 21710 Bayshore Road, Chestertown, MD 21620-4401, (410) 778-1982, msdbc@dmv.com,** or **www.mothersdaughters.org.**

How to Help Children through a Parent's Serious Illness by Kathleen McCue, MA, CCLS with Ron Bonn (St. Martin's Press, NY, 1994, $18.95). This practical

Lisa's Story

guide explains children's special needs when a parent is seriously ill. Provides guidelines, advice, and real-life examples to help parents and other caregivers help children during this stressful time. 221 pages. **Bookstores.**

"It Helps to Have Friends" (4654.00). A pamphlet for families with a parent who has cancer: Call the **ACS, (800) ACS-2345.**

Journaling through the Storm and *Silver Linings: The Other Side of Cancer* (Oncology Nursing Press, 1998). Companion volumes: an illustrated, colorful journal that invites the patient and her family to chronicle events, thoughts and feelings; and a collection of inspirational essays and poems. Purchase separately for $12.60/$19.50, or for $26.00 a special price for both volumes. Contact **ONS Customer Service, (412) 921-7373, customer.service@ons.org,** or **www.ons.org.**

The **Wellness Community** offers family support groups and family counseling through seventeen locations around the country. Contact the **Wellness Community Headquarters at 35 East 7th Street, Cincinnati, OH 45242, (888) 793-WELL,** or **www.cancer-support.org.**

Moms Don't Get Sick by Pat Brack with Ben Brack (Melius Publishing, Pierre, SD, 1990, $10.95). Told from a breast cancer patient's point of view and that of her ten-year-old son, this story covers over a year in the life of the Brack home and is "a story of anger, pain, hope and joy." 106 pages. Contact **Melius Publishing, 118 Riverroad, Pierre, South Dakota 57501, (800) 882-5171.**

Sammy's Mommy Has Cancer by Sherry Kohlenberg (Magination Press, NY, 1993, paperback/$8.95). The author, who was diagnosed with breast cancer

Resources

when she was thirty-four and her son was eighteen months old, offers parents a thoughtful and sensitive way to explain breast cancer to a child. Ms. Kohlenberg was a co-founder of the Virginia Breast Cancer Foundation and died in 1993. Thirty-two pages. **Bookstores, (800) 374-2721** or **www.maginationpress.com.**

"A Shared Purpose: A Guide for Daughters Whose Mothers Have Advanced Breast Cancer" (Cancer Care, 1998). Answers questions about advanced breast cancer, and anticipates feelings and emotions that mothers and daughters may face. Eighteen pages. Contact **Cancer Care, (800) 813-HOPE** or **www.cancercare.org.**

When a Parent Has Cancer: A Guide to Caring for Your Children with *Becky and the Worry Cup* by Wendy S. Harpham, M.D. (HarperCollins Publishers, New York, 1997, $24.00). The author, a lymphoma survivor, presents sensitive and practical advice to help children understand and cope with a parent's diagnosis of cancer. 164 pages. An illustrated children's book is included that tells the poignant story of Becky, a seven-year-old girl, and her experiences with her mother's cancer. Forty-six pages. **Bookstores.**

Family and Partner Issues: Resources for Children to Use

Caringkids is an Internet support group for children who know someone who is ill. It offers a monitored, open forum where kids may exchange information, share their feelings and make friends with other kids dealing with similar issues. To subscribe, go to **oncolink.upenn.edu/forms/listserv.html** (no "www" is needed).

Lisa's Story

Helping Children Cope Program of **Cancer Care, Inc.,** offers support groups and telephone counseling for children who have a parent with cancer. Contact **Cancer Care, Inc. (800) 813-HOPE,** or **www.cancercare.org.**

"Kemoshark" by H. Elizabeth King and illustrated by Diane Willford Steele (1995). A colorfully illustrated booklet to help children understand chemotherapy when their parents are undergoing treatment. Fourteen pages. Contact **KIDSCOPE, 3399 Peachtree Road, Suite 2020, Atlanta, GA 30326, (404) 233-0001,** or **www.kidscope.org.**

Kids Count Too is a six-session program of the **American Cancer Society** for preschool through teenage children who are coping with a parent's cancer. To find the program nearest you, contact the **ACS, (800) ACS-2345,** or **www.cancer.org.**

Kids Konnected is a support group for children whose mothers have breast cancer, run by the **Susan G. Komen Foundation.** To learn more, contact **(800) 899-2866,** or **www.kidskonnected.org.**

Kids Talk—Kids Speak Out About Breast Cancer by Laura Numeroff and Wendy S. Harpham, M.D., and illustrated by David McPhain (Samsung Telecommunications America and Sprint PCS, 1999). For children aged ten and younger, this book is composed of short stories told by children about living with a mother with breast cancer. Call the **Susan G. Komen Foundation, (800) I'M-AWARE.**

Mira's Month by Deborah Weinstein-Stern ($5.00). When the author's breast cancer recurred, she wrote this book for her four-year-old daughter, to help her cope while Mom was in the hospital for a month. It chronicles the events and feelings that a child experiences from the day she learns of her mother's cancer to the day she returns home from the hospital. Thirty-eight pages. Contact the **Blood and Marrow Transplant Newsletter** at **(847) 831-1913** or **(847) 831-1943** (fax).

The Paper Chain by Claire Blake, Eliza Blanchard, and Kathy Parkinson (Health Press, 1998). For children ages three to eight, this book relays the emotions of two young boys whose mom has breast cancer. The story includes the mother going to the hospital, having less energy for her sons and their changed lifestyle. The book encourages hope and open feelings. Thirty-two pages. **Bookstores.**

"When Someone in Your Family Has Cancer" (P619, 1995). An NCI booklet written for the child whose parent has cancer. It describes what cancer is, its treatment, and its emotional impact on family relationships. Includes a glossary of cancer-related terms. Twenty-eight pages. Call the **NCI's CIS, (800) 4-CANCER.**

COMPLEMENTS TO BREAST CANCER THERAPY— TREATING THE BODY AND SOUL

Diagnosis of and treatment for breast cancer is often a transforming experience—for the body, the emotions, and the soul. Many women have found it helpful to complement the treatment options of their choice with body work and other less traditional healing techniques. Here are a few ideas for the body and soul:

- **Massage therapy** by a qualified massage therapist experienced in working with breast cancer patients can make you more comfortable, relieve stress, and induce relaxation. Because of the need to treat the affected side and arm with care, the style of massage selected should be discussed with your physician. **The American**

Lisa's Story

Massage Therapy Association can refer you to members in your area who are AMTA-accredited, **(847) 864-0123** or **www.amtamassage.org.** Many states also require that therapists be licensed or pass a national certifying examination.

- **Retreats and getaways** designed for cancer survivors are increasingly available. **Casting for Recovery** offers an opportunity for survivors to learn fly-fishing on weekend retreats that focus on emotional and physical well-being. Call **CFR, (888) 553-3500** or **cfrprogram@aol.com.** The **Colorado Outward Bound School** offers a course specifically for women surviving cancer, **(888) 837-5204. Healing Adventures** sponsors outdoor adventures for people challenged by cancer, and for their friends and families, **(510) 237-8291. Wilderness Bay Wellness Foundation** designs and delivers therapeutic wilderness programs for female cancer patients and survivors, **(773) 334-0809.**

- **Visualization and imagery** are advocated by many as empowering tools against cancer that each person can summon and control. *Affirmations for Getting Well Again* (Touchstar Production, $24.95) is a guided imagery tape for patients who are undergoing cancer therapy. Thirty-eight minutes. Contact **Touchstar, (800) 759-1294** or **www.touchstarpro.com.**

- **Women in Nature** is an annual outdoor adventure in northern Minnesota for cancer survivors, **(612) 520-5157. Life Choices Wellness Center** offers seven-day retreats that include meditation and empowerment activities, **(800) 439-0083, lifechoices@lewcenter.com.** Two other programs are **Summits-Inner Mountain Wilderness Education Center, (907) 766-2074,** and **Expedition Inspiration** at **(208) 726-6456** or **www.expeditioninspiration.org.**

"**Breast Cancer and Sexuality**" (Cancer Care, 1998). A booklet that discusses sexuality, intimacy and menopausal symptoms. Fourteen pages. Contact **Cancer Care, (800) 813-HOPE** or **www.cancercare.org.**

Living in the Post-Mastectomy Body: Learning to Live in and Love Your Body Again by Becky Zuckweiler, M.S., R.N., C.S. (Hartley & Marks, Point Roberts, WA, 1998, paperback $19.95). The author, a nurse and psychotherapist who has had a double mastectomy, guides women through all aspects of recovery, focusing on regaining confidence in your body and developing a comfortable self-image and intimate relationships. **Bookstores.**

No Less a Woman: Femininity, Sexuality and Breast Cancer by Deborah Kahane, M.S.W. (Hunter House, Inc., Alameda, CA, 1995, Second Edition, paperback $14.95). This book, written by a breast cancer survivor, addresses the psycho-social and sexual impact that breast cancer has on the lives of women. Includes personal stories from several women and important resources. **Bookstores** or call **Hunter House, Inc., (800) 266-5592.**

"**Sexuality and Cancer: For the Woman Who Has Cancer, and Her Partner**" (4657, 1999 edition). Information about cancer, sexuality and areas of concern to the patient and her partner. Includes a resource list. Sixty-four pages. Call the **ACS, (800) ACS-2345.**

Sexuality and Fertility After Cancer by Leslie R. Schover, Ph.D. (John Wiley and Sons, Inc., New York, 1997, paperback, $15.95). Explains how treatment may emotionally and physically interfere with male and female sexual function

Lisa's Story

and fertility. As a resource, it helps survivors and their partners learn to enjoy sex again and make informed choices about having children. 304 pages. **Bookstores.**

6. Beyond Treatment and into Survivorship

A woman becomes a breast cancer survivor the moment after her diagnosis. With the advantages of early detection and current treatment, many women survive twenty years or longer post-diagnosis, and there are over two million women living in the United States today who have survived breast cancer. As more woman resume life after breast cancer—first marking months, then years—here are some action steps that will make a difference:

- *Talk it up.* Making continued progress against breast cancer will be easier if the subject remains in the spotlight.

- *Stay checked out, and tuned in.* Establish a schedule of checkups and mammograms with your surgeon or oncologist, and stick to it.

- *Get involved.* Join the growing breast cancer political advocacy movement on the local, state or national level, continuing the successful efforts started by patients and survivors in the early 1990's.

- *Support the cause.* Local and national nonprofit organizations need your financial support.

Living a Healthy Lifestyle: Diet

American Institute for Cancer Research provides information on cancer and nutrition. AICR publishes a newsletter, cookbooks and a series of diet/nutrition brochures. To order written materials or a publications list, contact **AICR, 1759 R Street, NW, Washington, DC 20009**, or **www.aicr.org**. In addition, AICR offers a hot line for nutrition-related cancer inquiries where callers will be connected with a registered dietitian, **(800) 843-8114**.

The Cancer Recovery Eating Plan: The Right Foods to Help Fuel Your Recovery by Daniel W. Nixon, M.D. (Random House, New York, 1996, paperback $15.00). A useful guide about what to eat after a cancer diagnosis, with a three-month eating plan, and more than one hundred recipes. 451 pages. **Bookstores.**

Low Fat and Loving It by Ruth Spear (Warner Books, New York, 1990, paperback $12.99). A healthy and creative approach to cooking by food author and NABCO co-founder. Over 200 recipes, plus information on the diet-cancer link, fat and cholesterol. Includes an easy-to-follow daily plan. 318 pages. **Bookstores.**

"How to Take Charge of Your Breast Health" (NABCO, May 2000). This brochure, produced jointly with Weight Watchers®, encourages a healthy lifestyle through diet and exercise, and suggests ways that women might lower their risk. Contact **NABCO, (800) 80-NABCO**, or **www.nabco.org**.

Living a Healthy Lifestyle: Exercise Videos

Better Than Before Fitness (1995, $39.95 plus $5.95 shipping). A video with exercises designed to restore muscle tone and full range of motion after breast

Lisa's Story

cancer surgery. Fifty minutes. Contact **Better Than Before Fitness, Ltd., (800) 488-8354,** or **www.breastfit.com.**

Focus on Healing Through Movement & Dance (Sherry Lebed Davis/Albert Einstein Medical Center, PA, $29.75 plus tax and $3.00 shipping). Now on video, a movement program and fourteen-day plan for breast cancer survivors of all ages and fitness levels. Helps regain full range of motion, reduce risk of lymphedema and improve self-image. Call **Enhancement, Inc., (888) 584-9633.**

Get Up and Go After Breast Surgery is an exercise video with sections on Reach to Recovery, Warm-up, Wall and Pole, Stretch and Tone and Meditation. ($39.95 plus $3.50 shipping). Sixty minutes. Call **Health Tapes, (800) 888-5236.**

One Move at a Time: Exercise for Women Recovering from Breast Cancer (Green Light Productions, Minneapolis, MN, 1996, $19.95 plus $4.45 shipping). A video with simple, gentle exercise to restore range of motion and aid in the recovery of feeling in the arm. Twenty-three minutes. Contact **The Cancer Club, 6533 Limerick Drive, Edina, MN 55439, (800) 586-9062,** or **www.cancerclub.com.**

EXERCISE AND BREAST CANCER

Researchers are continuing to explore the effect that **healthy lifestyles** can have on reducing breast cancer risk. Exercising regularly is one aspect of a healthy lifestyle. Work out, do aerobics, bike or even walk briskly—exercise to get your heart rate up, three or more times a week. Although several studies have shown that regular vigorous exercise lowers breast cancer risk, still to be discovered are the reasons why.

In addition to the video and written materials listed here, the **YWCA of the USA ENCOREplus Program** offers women recovering from breast cancer support and exercise groups focusing on physical strength, health and psychological well-being. Water toning and pool work are stressed. Call your local YWCA for more information, or call the **YWCA Office of Women's Health Initiatives, 624 9th Street, NW, Washington, DC 20001, (202) 628-3636.** In your own community, inquire at your physician's office, women's health clinic or at local hospitals for referrals to qualified personal trainers or fitness centers.

Living a Healthy Lifestyle: Managing Menopausal Symptoms

Dr. Susan Love's Hormone Book: Making Informed Choices About Menopause by Susan M. Love, M.D., with Karen Lindsey (Random House, New York, 1997, $25.00). Dr. Love's most recent book offers information on menopause and coping with symptoms, and addresses concerns about breast cancer. Includes a list of helpful resources. 362 pages. **Bookstores.**

Menopause by Richard J. Santen, M.D., Margaret Borwhat, and Sarah Gleason (The Hormone Foundation, Bethesda, MD, 1998). Summary of a 1997 meeting that discussed various ways to identify and treat symptoms of post-menopausal hormone deficiency in patients surviving breast cancer. Provides information for women on estrogen treatment, heart disease and breast cancer. Thirty pages. Contact **The Hormone Foundation, (800) HORMONE,** or **www.hormone.org.**

Without Estrogen: Natural Remedies for Menopause and Beyond by Dee Ito (Random House, Inc., New York, 1995, paperback $12.00). Offers options for managing the symptoms of menopause for women who cannot or choose not to rely on hormone replacement therapy. 246 pages. **Bookstores.**

Lisa's Story

Survivorship Resources

The Cancer Survivor's Toolbox is a self-learning audio program developed by leading national experts that focuses on six key skills to help survivors, family members and caregivers. Also available in Spanish and Mandarin Chinese. Free to survivors and professionals, call **(877) TOOLS-4-U.**

"Facing Forward: A Guide for Cancer Survivors" (P119, 1994). This guide from the NCI addresses the special needs of cancer survivors and their families, focusing on maintaining physical health, addressing emotional concerns, managing insurance issues and resolving employment problems: Forty-four pages. Call the **NCI's CIS, (800) 4-CANCER.**

Living Beyond Breast Caner: A Survivor's Guide for When Treatment Ends and the Rest of Your Life Begins by Marisa C. Weiss, M.D., and Ellen Weiss (Times Books, New York, 1997, $27.50). Written by the physician, founder and president of **Living Beyond Breast Cancer,** a nonprofit educational organization. A straightforward guide on adjusting to life after treatment. Topics include long-term side effects of treatment, employment and insurance issues and sexuality. **Bookstores.**

National Cancer Survivors' Day is America's nationwide, annual celebration of life for cancer survivors, their families, friends and oncology teams, celebrated on the first Sunday in June each year. For more information contact **National Cancer Survivors Day Foundation, P.O. Box 682285, Franklin, TN 37068-2285, (615) 794-3006,** or **www.ncsdf.org.**

The National Coalition for Cancer Survivorship (NCCS) raises awareness of cancer survivorship through its publications, quarterly newsletter, education to eliminate the stigma of cancer, and advocacy for insurance, employment, and legal rights for people with cancer. NCCS also facilitates networking among cancer programs, serves as an information clearinghouse and encourages the study of cancer survivorship. On a national level, NCCS provides public policy leadership on legislative, regulatory and financing matters and promotes responsible advocacy among national cancer organizations. For more information, contact **NCCS** at **1010 Wayne Avenue, Suite 505, Silver Spring, MD 20910, (877) 622-7937,** or **www.cansearch.org.**

To Be Alive: A Woman's Guide to a Full Life After Cancer by Carolyn D. Runowicz, M.D., and Donna Haupt (Henry Holt and Company, New York, 1996, hardcover $22.50, paperback $14.95). Written by a noted oncologist who is also a breast cancer survivor, this book offers the advice, reassurance, and support female cancer survivors need to resume a joyful and healthful life. Includes first-hand accounts of women who have completed cancer treatment and are on the road to recovery. 237 pages. **Bookstores.**

Waking Up, Fighting Back: The Politics of Breast Cancer by Roberta Altman (Little, Brown and Company, 1996, hardcover $24.45). An award-winning journalist's provocative survey of the issues and controversies of the breast cancer advocacy movement. 421 pages. **Bookstores.**

Lisa's Story

National Cancer and Breast Cancer Organizations

Contact the following national cancer and breast cancer organizations to learn more about their individual missions and how you can support their programs. All accept financial contributions.

- The **National Alliance of Breast Cancer Organizations (NABCO)** is the leading non-profit central resource for information and education about breast cancer, and a network of more than 400 organizations providing detection, treatment and care of American women. Founded in 1986, NABCO offers information, assistance and referral to anyone with questions about breast cancer, educates the public about the disease, links underserved women to medical services and acts as a voice for the interests and concerns of breast cancer survivors and women at risk. For more information, contact **NABCO, 9 East 37th Street, 10th Floor, New York, NY 10016, (888) 80-NABCO,** or **www.nabco.org.**

- The **American Cancer Society** has voluntary programs concerned with breast cancer in its divisions and units nationwide as well as national programs in research and advocacy. The ACS toll-free hot line, **(800) ACS-2345,** provides information on all forms of cancer and referrals to the ACS-sponsored "Reach to Recovery" and "Look Good, Feel Better" programs. For more information, contact your local American Cancer Society office or visit **www.cancer.org.**

- The **Breast Cancer Research Foundation,** founded in 1993 by Evelyn Lauder of the Estee Lauder Companies, Inc., funds clinical and genetic research at outstanding medical centers nationwide. For more information, contact the **Breast Cancer Research Foundation, 654 Madison Avenue, Suite 1209, New York, NY 10021, (646) 497-2600,** or **www. bcrfcure.org.**

- The **National Breast Cancer Coalition (NBCC)** is a grassroots advocacy organization committed to the eradication of the breast cancer epidemic. Conceived in 1991, NBCC numbers more than 450 member organizations and 58,000 individual members. The NBCC's goals are: research—increasing appropriations for high quality, peer-reviewed research and working within the scientific community to focus research on prevention and finding a cure; access—increasing access for all women to high quality treatment and care and to breast cancer clinical trials; and influence—increasing the influence of women living with breast cancer and other breast cancer activists in the decision-making that impacts all issues surrounding breast cancer. For more information, contact **NBCC, 1707 L Street, NW, Suite 1060, Washington, DC 20036, (202) 296-7477,** or **www.natl bcc.org.**

- Established in 1982, **The Susan G. Komen Breast Cancer Foundation**'s mission is to eradicate breast cancer as a life-threatening disease by advancing research, education, screening and treatment. A network of volunteers and one of the nation's largest private funders of breast cancer research, the Komen Foundation has raised in excess of $136 million since its inception. For more information, contact the **Susan G. Komen Breast Cancer Foundation, 5005 LBJ Freeway, Suite 370, Dallas, TX 75244, (800) I'M AWARE,** or **www.breastcancer info.com.**

- **Y-ME National Breast Cancer Organization** provides breast cancer information, support, and referrals through its national twenty-four hour toll-free hot lines: English **(800) 221-2141** and Spanish **(800) 986-9505.** Y-ME's hot lines are staffed by trained peer counselors who are all breast cancer survivors. Y-ME

Lisa's Story

has a hot line for men, Latina services, educational and advocacy programs and more than twenty chapters nationwide. The National Office can provide information on establishing affiliated groups. Contact, **Y-ME, 212 W. Van Buren, 5th Floor, Chicago, IL 60607, (800) 221-2141,** or **www.y-me.org.**